# MAKING INTEGRATED CURRICULUM WORK

TEACHERS, STUDENTS, AND THE QUEST

FOR COHERENT CURRICULUM

# MAKING INTEGRATED CURRICULUM WORK

## TEACHERS, STUDENTS, AND THE QUEST FOR COHERENT CURRICULUM

**P. ELIZABETH PATE**
*The University of Georgia, Athens, GA*

**ELAINE R. HOMESTEAD**
*Duluth Middle School, Duluth, GA*

**KAREN L. McGINNIS**
*Duluth Middle School, Duluth, GA*

Foreword by
JAMES A. BEANE

Teachers College, Columbia University
New York and London

Published by Teachers College Press, 1234 Amsterdam Avenue, New York, N.Y. 10027

*Library of Congress Cataloging-in-Publication Data*

Pate, P. Elizabeth.
    Making integrated curriculum work : teachers, students, and the
quest for coherent curriculum / P. Elizabeth Pate, Elaine R.
Homestead, Karen L. McGinnis ; foreword by James A. Beane
        p.   cm.
    Includes bibliographical references and index.
    ISBN 0-8077-3597-3 (paper : alk. paper). — ISBN 0-8077-3598-1 (cloth :
alk. paper)
        1. Middle schools—United States—curricula. 2. Interdisciplinary
approach in education—United States.   I. Homestead, Elaine R.,
1947-   . II. McGinnis, Karen L., 1963-   . III. Title
    LB1628.5.P38  1996
    373.19—dc20                                          96-42444
ISBN 0-8077-3597-3 (paper)
ISBN 0-8077-3598-1 (cloth)


Printed on acid-free paper
Manufactured in the United States of America
04  03  02  01  00  99  98  97      8  7  6  5  4  3  2  1

# Contents

*Foreword by James A. Beane*     ix
*Preface: Essential Components of Coherent Curriculum*     xiii

Chapter 1     The McHome Team                                              1

Chapter 2     Component: Goals                                             6
              *Teacher Beliefs, Theories, and Goals  6*
              *Conclusion   10*

Chapter 3     Component: Democratic Classroom                            15
              *Management Plan   17*
              *Group Processing   23*
              *Grading Policy   24*
              *Group-Work Guidelines   27*
              *Conclusion   28*

Chapter 4     Component: Traditional and Alternative Assessment          31
              *Curriculum Design Process   33*
              *Rubrics   38*
              *Assessment Examples   40*
              *Conclusion   43*

Chapter 5     Component: Content Integration                             46
              *Modeling Integration of Content   48*
              *Integrating Content Within Thematic Units   53*
              *Conclusion   59*

Chapter 6     Component: Pedagogy                                        60
              *Strategy: Brainstorming   60*
              *Strategy: Making Connections   61*
              *Strategy: Storytelling   63*
              *Strategy: Making Connections   63*
              *Strategy: Jigsaw   64*
              *Strategy: Data Retrieval Chart   64*

*Strategy: Simulation   66*
*Strategy: Making Connections   66*
*Strategy: Collaborative Problem Solving   67*
*Conclusion   67*

Chapter 7    Component: Communication                                    68
*Communication with Students   68*
*Communication with Parents   70*
*Student Communication with Others   71*
*Teacher Communication with Others   74*
*Conclusion   74*

Chapter 8    Component: Scheduling and Organizational Structures    75
*Two-Teacher Team   75*
*Team Teaching   77*
*Class Schedules   78*
*Classroom Organization   79*
*Conclusion   79*

Chapter 9    Component: Reflection   80
*Examples of the Reflection Process   80*
*Conclusion   107*

Chapter 10   Communities of the Future                                  108
*Initial Unit Preparation   109*
*Content Instruction   111*
*Determining Communities   114*
*Development and Presentation of Communities   115*

Chapter 11   Continuing the Quest                                       134

*References*                                                            *141*

*Index*                                                                 *145*

*About the Authors*                                                     *149*

*This book is dedicated to:*
*our McHome Team students,*
*our husbands Steve Pate, Tom Homestead, and Jimmy McGinnis,*
*James Beane,*
*and others involved in curriculum reform.*

# Foreword

## THINKING FOR OURSELVES

Almost every teacher has been confronted by students asking, "why do we have to learn this?" "What is this for?" "When will we ever use this?" In fact, such questions are so common that they need little explanation to argue for designing learning experiences that are meaningful and relevant for young people. Rarely, though, do we hear of teachers raising similar questions from their side of the desk: "Why do I have to teach this?" "What is this for?" "When will they ever use this?" It is easy to forget that the external curriculum mandates and traditional school structures that appear to constrict the lives and learning of young people have the same effect on their teachers.

Certainly not all teachers object to external curriculum mandates or to the rigid structures of schooling that develop around them. Some welcome both, perhaps because rules and regulations give an air of authority to the teacher or because the difficult work of teaching is made a bit easier if others decide what should be taught and how. Furthermore, some teachers are eager participants on committees seeking to standardize content and pedagogy from the national to the local level. And their participation helps legitimate the countless bureaucrats, academicians, and politicians who seem to love nothing more than the possibility of exercising ever greater control over what happens in classrooms, while not having to spend more than a photo opportunity inside one. It is almost as if many of the participants in this kind of activity, including teachers, actually believe that by creating greater external control over curriculum and teaching that the problems of education will go away, including the student and teacher questions about why particular things are taught.

Meanwhile, some teachers are seeking a quite different path to answering their students' and their own questions about the purpose and relevance of the curriculum. Rather than relying only on outside sources for curriculum decisions and justifications, these teachers are also turning to their students and to their own professional judgment to create possibilities for curriculum and teaching. Among these teachers are Elaine Homestead and Karen McGinnis, who along with a professor, Elizabeth Pate, undertook a year long search for ways to create what they came to call a "coherent curriculum." This book is an account of that search.

What makes this book most intriguing is that it can be read for multiple meanings. For example, while most authors on the topic of coherence focus on learning theory, the emphasis here is on the teachers' thinking as they constructed their theory of coherence through deliberation, action, and reflection. In this way the book could stand alone as an example of the kind of reflective teacher research that is presently breathing fresh air into the generally abstract and aloof world of educational inquiry.

*Making Integrated Curriculum Work* might also be read for its unusual theoretical meanings. For example, the idea of coherence emerges as a unified framework of progressive teaching methods including an issue-based curriculum, collaborative planning with students, integration of knowledge, authentic assessment, and democratic governance. Integration of knowledge emerges as the simultaneous use of student concerns, external mandates, social issues, popular culture, and other sources of inquiry and knowledge, and including both content and skill within that broad mix.

On a third level, this book might be read as a sourcebook on teaching methods. As the search for a coherent curriculum unfolds, we are given numerous examples of how we might plan with students and involve them in classroom governance, how to communicate with parents, how to assess student work in a project-based approach, how to organize teacher planning, and more. Just as importantly, those methods are described here not by teachers for whom they are simply routine procedures but by teachers who are searching for a better way to help their students learn. For this reason, in fact, the book might stand alone for those who are willing to try some progressive teaching but are not altogether sure how to get started.

For me, though, the book has yet another meaning. The authors claim early on that they were partly motivated to carry out their "quest" after reading some of the writing I had done on curriculum integration, especially as that involved planning with students. Yet the way in which they went about that work was quite different from the way I had as I worked alongside teachers in my home school district. Not only that, but their way was also different from that of still other teachers I know who also claimed to start in the same place.

Among the many meanings in the book, this one may be the most important: As teachers pursue a common agenda for a more progressive and coherent curriculum, there may be many ways that agenda might be brought to life. Moreover, it is exactly out of such diversity that a rich curriculum conversation might develop in which all of us might learn from one another. For this reason, just as I want to immediately congratulate Elizabeth, Elaine, and Karen for their wonderful work, I also want to ask them a thousand questions about why they did one or another thing the way they did.

The only trouble with the conversations that ensue from such questions is that we sometimes forget how they started; namely by someone having the courage to take action. And so, as we read and reflect on this book, we should not forget that in the popular rush to find curriculum decisions and justifications outside the classroom, there are still teachers, many in fact, who understand the importance of looking inside as well—inside, to their own professional judgment and to the young people with whom they work. Thankfully there is a growing body of literature by and about these teachers. And thankfully this book, *Making Integrated Curriculum Work,* is among them.

*James A. Beane*
*National-Louis University*

# Preface

## ESSENTIAL COMPONENTS OF COHERENT CURRICULUM

Recently we, Karen and Elaine (two middle school teachers) and Elizabeth (an associate professor of middle school education), embarked on a quest in discovery of coherent curriculum. To us, a coherent curriculum encompasses meeting the needs of students and teachers, connecting the content, encouraging student voice, and relating schooling to real life, thereby ensuring that student learning is relevant and personally meaningful.

The quest began because of our, Elaine's and Karen's, dissatisfaction with teaching on a traditional middle school interdisciplinary team and with a curriculum that we felt was not meeting the needs of our students. We also wanted to respond to calls for education reform from parents, educators, and leaders of the working community.

In preparation, the three of us first met to discuss curriculum issues, teaming, scheduling, teaching and learning strategies, and student and teacher motivation. Reading extensively helped develop our own understanding of what makes a curriculum coherent.

The quest began with making significant changes in how we all thought about teaching and learning. As a result, Elaine and Karen established the McHome Team, a two-teacher, eighth-grade team in a suburban middle school in Georgia. Developing a democratic classroom, one in which students are actively involved in decision making, with our 58 students was a top priority. Implementing integrated curriculum was not left to chance but actively pursued. Weeks and sometimes months were devoted to thematic units such as Human Migration, Human Interactions, Human Interactions and the Environment, Human and Civil Rights and Responsibilities, Leadership, and Communities of the Future. Block scheduling was implemented to better meet the needs of all involved. Advisor–advisee relationships (making time for teachers and students to talk about students' social and emotional needs and concerns) were embedded within this block of time.

This book tells the story of our quest for coherent curriculum. Through the detailed description of our year-long journey, eight essential components of a coherent curriculum emerge. It is important to note that even though the components are discussed separately (in Chapters 2 through 9), in reality they are intertwined. It is also important to recognize that integrated curriculum looks different in every classroom and across years.

Chapter 1 is the story of the McHome Team. This chapter provides an overview of our 18-month quest. In Chapter 2, we provide an explanation of how and why the McHome Team goals were determined. Goals are an important component of coherent curriculum in that they guide the curriculum, shape how it is taught and learned, and provide a sense of purpose to schooling. In this chapter our goals are shared. Some examples of our goals include developing a curriculum in which students and teachers have a deeper understanding of content, encouraging student acceptance of responsibilities, and teaching students how to learn.

In Chapter 3, we discuss how our team created a democratic classroom. Having a democratic classroom was extremely important in our quest for a coherent curriculum. Democracy on the McHome Team included student and teacher collaboration on such things as our team management plan, our grading policy, parent communication, and development of our integrated curriculum. We provide the reader with a day-by-day account of how our democratic classroom evolved. This chapter also includes students' comments regarding their perceptions of a democratic classroom.

Assessment was an integral part of our coherent curriculum. Chapter 4 describes how we matched assessments to themes, activities, and the needs of our students. Student-generated and teacher-generated examples of assessment are provided. In addition, students share their perceptions of traditional and alternative assessments.

Chapter 5 details how we integrated content within themes. After elaborating on what we mean by the concept of content, we share the design process used in the development of our thematic units as well.

Chapter 6 is a discussion of our pedagogy. Appropriate pedagogy connects the curriculum to the needs of the student. Examples of specific strategies used in our Human and Civil Rights and Responsibilities unit are provided.

In Chapter 7, we discuss communication. Integrated curriculum, because it was unfamiliar to students, parents, and many administrators, required open and frequent communication. Rationale, examples, and formats of effective communication are presented and discussed.

In Chapter 8, we discuss block scheduling, task-specific scheduling, effective classroom organization, and the changing physical setting of the classroom. The rationale for a two-teacher team is also presented.

Reflection means to stop and look back. What worked? What didn't work? What did we learn? In Chapter 9, we provide our rationale for reflection, show how we modeled reflecting with the students, and discuss the importance of group processing. We also present examples of how we reflected daily, at the end of each 6 weeks, and at the end of the school year. How we developed our eight essential components of a coherent curriculum is also shared.

Chapter 10 is a detailed account of how our team worked collaboratively to create coherent curriculum. In Chapter 11, we make a proposal for middle school curriculum changes, taking into consideration historical curriculum accounts, current curriculum integration efforts, as well as our own quest for coherent curriculum.

We believe that this book is for all persons interested in young adolescents and their schooling. The experiences shared are meant to provide further insight into what coherent curriculum is and what it looked like on one eighth-grade team. We hope that what we have written about our quest for coherent curriculum adds to the reader's thoughts on curriculum reform.

# Chapter 1

# THE McHOME TEAM

In the spring of 1992, Karen and Elaine were on a five-member eighth-grade interdisciplinary team in a middle school in the suburban Atlanta area. The ethnic mix of the school was approximately 90% Caucasian, 5% Asian, 3% African American, and 2% Hispanic. Most students were middle class and lived with two parents. Karen taught science and Elaine taught social studies. There were 150 students on our team. We considered ourselves lucky if we had learned all of the students' names by Thanksgiving, much less in which class period we saw the students. It was ridiculous to even think about meeting the "needs of the students."

The class periods were 45 minutes long. Only about 35 minutes of instructional time remained by the time the students arrived and administrative tasks were taken care of. This was not enough time to get involved in meaningful learning. Because of the size of the team, exploratory classes, lunch schedules, and other special-needs programs, there was little flexibility in scheduling our class periods. Since the students rotated from class to class, day in and day out, their interest was hard to get and maintain, and enthusiasm for school was low.

Teaching approximately the same lesson five times a day left us discontented. Even though we were on a five-teacher interdisciplinary team, our disciplines rarely connected. We felt conflict between our philosophy and our practice.

As a result of this conflict, we read anything we could get our hands on about interdisciplinary instruction, integrating the curriculum, alternative assessments, and other educational innovations. Some of the literature we read included Beane (1991, 1992), Brandt (1991, 1992), Capelluti &

Brazee (1992), Carnegie Council on Adolescent Development (1989), Dewey (1915, 1938), Fogarty (1991), Glasser (1986), Jacobs (1989, 1991), Lounsbury (1991), Merenbloom (1991), Schlechty (1991), Spady & Marshall (1991), Toepfer (1992a), Vars (1991), Wiggins (1992), and Wigginton (1986). We were entranced by our readings and began to discuss how we could use this information to create a coherent curriculum.

Our advisor and instructor during graduate studies at TheUniversity of Georgia was Elizabeth. At the time, she was working with the Delta Team (Pate, Mizelle, Hart, Jordan, R. Matthews, S. Matthews, Scott, and Brantley), an eight-teacher team from a rural middle school in Georgia, on a long-term study of teacher/student progression. The Delta Team was just wrapping up the second year of their 3-year cycle. Elizabeth was aware of our interest in learning more about innovative programs for middle schools and arranged for us to visit the Delta Team. We spent the day observing them working with their students. We also made time to share ideas and educational philosophies. During these conversations, the Delta Team mentioned James Beane's (1990) book, *A Middle School Curriculum: From Rhetoric to Reality,* as being influential in shaping their philosophy of what a middle school curriculum should be. We scanned the book and were intrigued by what we read. We each bought a copy of the book and read it from cover to cover. When thinking back, it is clear to us that reading *this* book was a pivotal point in our lives as educators of young adolescents. It brought together for all of us the seemingly disparate elements of a middle school (interdisciplinary teaming, block scheduling, advisor–advisee programs, exploratory programs) into a meaningful whole. A picture of a coherent curriculum began to emerge.

Prior to reading *A Middle School Curriculum: From Rhetoric to Reality,* our focus had been on *what was being taught.* Content delivery was the primary consideration in every decision we had previously made to improve our teaching. We now began to focus on *what was being learned and by whom.* It seemed clear that all decisions made at the middle school level should be based on what we know about the social needs, emotional needs, motivational needs, and physical needs—not just the cognitive needs—of the middle school learner. In other words, we should consider the whole child. As Beane (1990) stated, the middle school movement has made great strides in restructuring almost every aspect of the middle school *except curriculum.* We were committed to making our curriculum responsive to the interests and needs of our students, as well as maintaining academically challenging standards.

At this same time, our school district was in the process of restructuring. The county office was encouraging teachers to try new and innovative ideas. This was the perfect time to try a new program.

In May 1992, we wrote a proposal to our principal that included our rationale for asking for a two-teacher team, the purpose of our new program, and a model of the instructional day. Our proposal was accepted. Each of us would teach a traditional math skills class. The rest of the 3-hour academic block time would be uninterrupted. The only drawback we faced was that our classrooms were across the hall from each other. We would have to crowd all 58 students into one room whenever we wanted to have team meetings or large-group instruction.

During that spring, Elizabeth helped us develop a survey for the incoming eighth graders. We wanted to use their responses to help personalize learning. We asked the students to tell us how they learned best, what concerned them the most at school, what they would like to learn, and what they would change about school if they could. The survey revealed that the students wanted less "book work" and more projects. They wanted to study more about current issues and less about what happened a long time ago.

During the summer, the three of us conceptualized a framework for an integrated curriculum for the 1992–1993 school year. We decided to develop themes using social studies as the organizer. We felt it was easier to integrate the disciplines into social studies because it seemed to be the most flexible. We developed loose frameworks for integration of content into the themes, realizing that things would change as soon as there was student input.

Structuring our program to meet the social, emotional, motivational, and physical needs of our students, and not just focusing on their cognitive development, was a major shift in curriculum development for us. We spent a great deal of time discussing the supporting structures that we felt were necessary for curriculum integration: setting goals, developing a democratic classroom, encouraging student–teacher collaboration, and providing for effective communication.

At the beginning of the 1992–1993 school year, the McGinnis–Homestead (McHome) Team consisted of 58 students and ourselves. Of the students, 26 were boys and 32 were girls. There were 51 Caucasian, two African American, two Hispanic, and three Asian students.

Our school-day schedule began with a homeroom period from 7:30 to 7:40. During this time we took roll, prepared absentee reports, and listened to daily announcements over the public address system. We each taught a math class from 7:45 to 8:35. From 8:40 to 10:30, the students had exploratory classes (physical education, art, chorus, orchestra, band, health, current events, career exploration, technology education, home economics education, computer education, or foreign language). At 10:35, students returned to our classrooms for the remainder of the day.

The first 2 weeks of school were spent getting to know each other and establishing a democratic classroom. We began by introducing ourselves and sharing personal information with our team and encouraging our students to do the same. Survey responses that we had collected from them the previous spring were discussed. We shared our vision of the school year and how it would be different from previous school years.

The remainder of the school year was devoted to our quest for coherent curriculum. We collaborated with our students on developing thematic units. The units included Human Migration, Human Interactions, Human Interactions and the Environment, Human and Civil Rights and Responsibilities, Leadership, and Communities of the Future.

We chose Human Migration as our first thematic unit of study. As we designed this unit, an effort was made to integrate all appropriate content. We developed this first unit ourselves instead of waiting for input from our students for several reasons: (1) we wanted to make sure we could teach content within a theme, (2) we wanted to find out if the central focus of social studies would work, (3) we wanted to model integrated curriculum for our students, and (4) we wanted to have something planned to begin the school year.

Our next thematic unit was Human Interactions. This unit was to be a study of social issues and concerns that affected us personally, as well as issues that have affected societies in the past. As we began to discuss the framework and expectations of this unit, our students became excited about the possibilities of being able to study the social and political issues about which they felt very strongly. They wanted to investigate such issues as racism, abortion rights, animal testing, and world hunger and then share their knowledge with others beyond the classroom. The students developed questions for research, determined how they would share their information with others, kept journals, and constructed their own assessments.

Our students were so interested in their study of current social issues affecting them that they wanted to continue their studies to include environmental issues of personal concern. So, we had a spin-off unit. In this spin-off unit, Human Interactions and the Environment, students chose topics to study. Their topics included such issues as ozone pollution, erosion due to clear cutting ("selective harvesting"), acid rain, and quality of air and water.

The democratic process became evident in our next unit, Human and Civil Rights and Responsibilities. In this unit we examined the relationships between past, present, and future human and civil rights issues from the 1600s to the present.

Our next unit, Leadership, developed into a novel study of *Jurassic Park* (Crichton, 1990). The students were tired and requested a break from research and group projects.

The final unit of the year was Communities of the Future. This unit incorporated the social studies concepts of governmental and economic systems and the science concepts found in the study of astronomy. This unit required the students to thoughtfully include content and apply skills learned from the other units we studied throughout the year.

Throughout the school year we were involved in action research. Student data we collected included interviews, written responses to questions, student-generated evaluations, journals, curriculum products, and videotapes of classroom discourse. Teacher data we collected included journals, curriculum artifacts, and audiotaped discussions.

The summer of 1993 was a time of reflection. We asked ourselves, "What are the elements we think are necessary for successful curriculum integration?" After much discussion, we spread out long sheets of paper and developed a chart. This chart eventually became our tool for identifying the components of coherent curriculum: goals, democratic classroom, traditional and alternative assessments, content integration, pedagogy, communication, scheduling and organizational structures, and reflection.

# Chapter 2

# COMPONENT: GOALS

As stated in the McHome Team chapter, we began our quest for coherent curriculum by questioning our beliefs about adolescents, curriculum, and schooling. Clark and Peterson (1986), in their review of research on teacher thinking, generated a Model of Teachers' Thought and Action. This model describes relationships between teachers' actions and their thought processes. Three basic dimensions of thought processes were identified: planning, theories and beliefs, and interactive thoughts and decisions. According to Clark and Peterson, theories and beliefs sometimes shape actions and, as a result of actions, teachers sometimes modify their theories and beliefs. This is exactly what happened to us during our quest for coherent curriculum. We examined our beliefs as well as educational theories; we made changes in what we taught, how we taught, and how we assessed; and we ultimately modified or refined our beliefs.

In this chapter we discuss educational theories that guided our thinking regarding educating young adolescents. We discuss our own beliefs connected to these theories and we share how these beliefs translated into our McHome Team goals.

## TEACHER BELIEFS, THEORIES, AND GOALS

As we thought about middle school education, we took into account our own personal beliefs as well as educational theories about schooling. Our overarching goal for the year was to integrate the curriculum for a team of 58 eighth graders. Our whole way of thinking about middle school curriculum changed. We believed in middle school curriculum integration theory. This theory "takes into account the particular views of young adolescents, the purpose of middle schools, the sources of the curriculum, the nature of learning, the contexts of knowledge and skill, and the organization of the curriculum" (Beane, 1993, p. 4).

We did not want to be "teachers" during our year of curriculum integration and coherent curriculum. Not once, as you can see in our goals, have we used the word *teach*. We were not teachers; rather, we viewed ourselves as instigators, "instigators of learning." We changed the context for learning from one that is teacher directed and planned to one of collaboration between students and teachers. Yinger (1980) characterized teacher planning as decision making based on problem solving. He described a cyclical process of problem finding, problem design, and problem evaluation. We extended this perspective during our quest for coherent curriculum. As curriculum collaborators, we (students and teachers) were engaged in problem finding (determining what was to be learned), problem design (determining how it was going to be learned), and problem evaluation (determining learning was going to be assessed).

In our quest for coherent curriculum, we considered how students learn. From the cognitive perspective, learning is the acquisition of knowledge; the ability to think and to process information. The cognitive constructivist view of learning takes into account the active personal role of students during learning and recall. According to Vygotsky (1978), cognitive development occurs for young adolescents when they interact with other people who provide the necessary support for learning to take place. Learning becomes a self-regulated process of resolving inner cognitive conflicts through concrete experiences, collaborative discourse, and reflection. Self-regulated learning fits with our belief that students should not be passive recipients of information, but rather, students should actively contribute to their learning goals. In other words, we felt that students should be active constructors of knowledge, rather than passive recipients of information. We wanted our students to gain knowledge (e.g., knowledge about themselves, knowledge about their world). We did not want our students to just gain information (e.g., the history of Georgia, the parts of speech). And we knew that learning is a social process. Students gain knowledge from each other and from adults.

We wanted to develop curriculum that focused on hands-on experimentation, learner-generated questions, investigations, and demonstrations of student learning. We believed in the five principles of a constructivist pedagogy as outlined by Brooks and Brooks (1993). These principles include:

1. Posing problems of emerging relevance to learners
2. Structuring learning around "big ideas" or primary concepts

3  Seeking and valuing students' points of view
4  Adapting curriculum to address students' suppositions
5. Assessing student learning in the context of teaching

Elaine stated that when she was a member of an interdisciplinary team
(four or five teachers teaching mathematics, science, reading, language arts,
and social studies in 50-minute class periods), she had forgotten much of
the curriculum herself. Upon reflection, she said:

> One year I taught Georgia Studies, four times a day. The next year I
> taught language arts, four times a day. Then I taught Georgia Studies
> again. I had forgotten so much of the curriculum in just one year. I
> came to the conclusion that covering the curriculum, even when you
> are teaching it, does not constitute an in-depth understanding of it. I
> felt that if I, the teacher, did not remember it, then how can I truly
> expect students to remember it. I started thinking, we have to decide
> what is important in the curriculum. What part of the curriculum
> facilitates helping kids know how to make sense of themselves?

Curriculum integration and motivation go hand in hand. Integrated curriculum provides experiences for students that are inherently compelling.
Because students are engaged in meaningful learning stemming from their
own interests and concerns, there is an intrinsic motivation to learn. Learning
comes from within, from the desire to satisfy curiosities and know more
about self and society. The process of learning then becomes as important
as what is being learned.

We wanted to find out what our students thought was the purpose of
schooling. Their response was "to prepare us to go to work to earn a living." We wanted school to be more than just a preparation for getting a
job. We wanted it to be meaningful for the students. Connections had to
be made for the students. We wanted our students to become empowered.
In order for school to have meaning, they had to accept responsibility for
their learning. We wanted them to have ownership in what they learned,
how they learned, and how they were assessed. We felt if students had ownership in their curriculum, then they in turn would be more motivated.

We wanted to guide our students in the learning process. We felt this
was important because we knew they would not be used to this type of
schooling (integrated curriculum). We wanted to model curriculum planning
for our students so they could begin to plan on their own. For example,
our first unit, Human Migration, was primarily teacher designed. The teachers planned the guidelines; students had input regarding choices of how they
wanted to learn and choices about assessment (see Chapter 5). Through scaf-

folding (model, coach, fade, transfer), our students gained the experiential background necessary for them to begin planning their own curriculum. Through this process, the students eventually changed from the traditional paradigm (teachers teaching) to a new paradigm (students and teachers creating the curriculum).

It is also our belief that students need to learn to work effectively with a diversity of people. We embraced the notion of multicultural education. Multicultural education is designed to give students a realistic perspective of the diversity of American culture, including the numerous ethnic groups as well as religious groups and their beliefs, the concerns of women today, the rights of children, and issues important to many other groups in the nation today (Tiedt & Tiedt, 1986). Dewey (1990, p. 12) suggested schools prepare students to have an "increase in toleration, in breadth of social judgment, the larger acquaintance with human nature, the sharpened alertness in reading signs of character and interpreting social situations, greater accuracy of adaptation to differing personalities, contact with greater commercial activities." These same beliefs that Dewey proposed helped guide our quest for coherent curriculum. Through integrated curriculum, we felt we would be providing rich and meaningful opportunities for students to learn about themselves and each other, leading to greater acceptance and understanding.

Knowledge often comes from making mistakes. Risk taking, therefore, is essential to make schooling meaningful. We realized that in order for our students to be problem solvers, they had to take risks and learn from mistakes. We felt that the deepest, longest-lasting learning comes from taking risks. Making mistakes often personalizes learning for students. We wanted our students to know that failing at something can be a positive experience if you learn from it. We wanted our curriculum to be built upon puzzling problems and creative ways to solve those problems.

We also believed that schooling should not only be meaningful, but fun as well. School should be associated with something pleasant. We did not want our students to consider school boring. We wanted our students to want to become life-long learners; to think of learning as fun and exciting.

Because of our beliefs, we developed the following long-term goals. We wanted to:

- Develop a curriculum that gives students and teachers a deeper understanding of content
- Make connections between school and the outside world
- Guide students in the learning process
- Encourage students to accept responsibilities
- Help students learn to work effectively with a diversity of people
- Encourage students to take risks and learn from mistakes

- Assist students in becoming effective problem solvers
- Enable students to discover that learning can be fun

## CONCLUSION

Ultimately, our quest for coherent curriculum was the type of sustained, student-centered curricula that recent reform proposals have advocated (Beane, 1995b; Carnegie Council On Adolescent Development, 1989; Middle Level Curriculum Project, 1991).

In our quest for coherent curriculum, we departed from the tradition of adapting the high school separate-subject curriculum model for use at the middle level. We ended up with curriculum that made sense to us all. Our curriculum took into account actual characteristics of middle school students. We did not believe the many popular litanies of the characteristics of young adolescents that often misrepresent them. Sometimes in middle schools, too much focus is placed on the "phases" a young adolescent goes through. Instead, we focused on who our students were and what and how they wanted to learn. And sometimes in middle schools, students are not given enough credit for what they can do and sometimes they are not challenged enough. In our quest for coherent curriculum, our students pushed themselves and were definitely challenged.

Our integrated, coherent curriculum was a general education program. We addressed questions and concerns that our students had about themselves and their world, as well as issues in the larger world of which our students may not have been aware. We found out what our students were interested in learning. Beane (1993) suggested that educators need to address the question: What do young adolescents want from schools—if they could have whatever they want? This ties in directly with our goal setting. We created our Survey of Rising Eighth Graders to determine our students' concerns (see Figure 2.1). The survey was given to the seventh-grade classes (approximately 274 students) in May 1992. The survey was loosely based on our reading of Beane's *A Middle School Curriculum: From Rhetoric to Reality*. The students were asked to answer 18 Likert-type questions and 3 short-answer questions. Not all students responded to all questions.

From the responses on the 18 Likert-type questions, it appeared that students were most concerned about their personal wellness, their opinions, their friends' feelings, understanding between races, respect for other people's cultural heritage/background, how they are perceived, and how their actions affect their teachers (see Figure 2.2).

The three short-answer questions provided a variety of answers as shown in Figure 2.3. The topics most frequently mentioned in response to

## Figure 2-1. Survey of Rising Eighth Graders

CIRCLE ONE: male   female      RACE: _____      AGE: _____

CIRCLE THE ANSWER THAT BEST DESCRIBES YOUR FEELINGS.

1. Do you ever worry about the physical changes you are going through?
   never          sometimes          often          always

2. Are you concerned with understanding your inner self (who you are)?
   never          sometimes          often          always

3. Are you concerned about being accepted in any social group?
   never          sometimes          often          always

4. Is your personal physical wellness important to you?
   never          sometimes          often          always

5. Do you ever have difficulty with adults understanding you?
   never          sometimes          often          always

6. Do you ever have difficulty understanding adults?
   never          sometimes          often          always

7. Are you interested in finding better ways to solve peer conflicts?
   never          sometimes          often          always

8. When everyone at school has the latest fashion and you don't, does this bother you?
   never          sometimes          often          always

9. Do you feel that you have the freedom to (respectfully) question adults at school?
   never          sometimes          often          always

10. Do you feel that rules are necessary?
    never          sometimes          often          always

11. Do you feel that your opinion counts at school?
    never          sometimes          often          always

12. Do you feel that your opinion counts at home?
    never          sometimes          often          always

13. Do you put your friends' feelings before your own?
    never          sometimes          often          always

14. Do you think we need more understanding between races at DMS?
    never          sometimes          often          always

15. Do you respect other people's cultural heritage/background?
    never          sometimes          often          always

16. Do you feel that you need to know the things about you that upset others?
    never          sometimes          often          always

*(continued)*

**Figure 2-1.** Survey of Rising Eighth Graders (cont'd.)

17. Do you feel that you need to know how your actions affect the way the teacher treats you?

    never            sometimes            often            always

18. Do you feel that you need to know how to make better decisions?

    never            sometimes            often            always

SHORT ANSWERS
  1. What is your #1 personal concern at DMS?
  2. What do you feel is most important that you learn next year to help you in the future?
  3. If you could change one thing about your academic subjects next year, what would it be?

---

**Figure 2-2.** Survey of Rising Eighth Graders: Results

|             | NEVER | SOMETIMES | OFTEN | ALWAYS |           |
|-------------|-------|-----------|-------|--------|-----------|
| Question 1  | 24%   | 65%       | 9%    | 2%     | n = 273   |
| Question 2  | 32%   | 45%       | 18%   | 5%     | n = 274   |
| Question 3  | 21%   | 39%       | 26%   | 14%    | n = 274   |
| Question 4  | 3%    | 17%       | 35%   | 45%    | n = 273   |
| Question 5  | 13%   | 45%       | 29%   | 13%    | n = 273   |
| Question 6  | 14%   | 55%       | 23%   | 8%     | n = 274   |
| Question 7  | 22%   | 47%       | 22%   | 9%     | n = 273   |
| Question 8  | 29%   | 46%       | 14%   | 11%    | n = 273   |
| Question 9  | 23%   | 36%       | 19%   | 22%    | n = 271   |
| Question 10 | 8%    | 43%       | 24%   | 25%    | n = 270   |
| Question 11 | 24%   | 27%       | 22%   | 27%    | n = 273   |
| Question 12 | 7%    | 19%       | 32%   | 42%    | n = 273   |
| Question 13 | 4%    | 46%       | 38%   | 12%    | n = 270   |
| Question 14 | 10%   | 34%       | 27%   | 29%    | n = 267   |
| Question 15 | 5%    | 20%       | 39%   | 36%    | n = 205   |
| Question 16 | 7%    | 25%       | 31%   | 37%    | n = 268   |
| Question 17 | 9%    | 31%       | 32%   | 28%    | n = 272   |
| Question 18 | 13%   | 47%       | 25%   | 15%    | n = 273   |

**Figure 2-3.** Survey of Rising Eighth Graders:
Sample Responses to Short Answers

1. What is your #1 *personal* concern at DMS?:
   - I'm just afraid of messing up or failing and not being able to turn back & fix my mistakes.
   - Friends.
   - Racism.
   - The administrators need to ask the whole student body to make decisions.
   - Not fitting in.
   - How to treat each other equally.
   - Getting along with others and adults.
   - The hazards that we put in the environment, from construction.
   - Socialization.

2. What do you feel is most important that you learn next year to help you in the future?:
   - How to have good study skills.
   - Responsibility.
   - How to solve problems.
   - Learn to work and cooperate with others.
   - Decisions, careers, and social life.
   - Help teens get out of a bad situation.
   - We need some time to reach our point to learn.
   - Peer conflicts.
   - How to get along with others and adults.
   - Computers.
   - Self-discipline.

3. If you could change one thing about your academic subjects next year, what would it be?:
   - I would like it to be more democratic.
   - For it not to be so much out of the book and more hands on so we're not so bored to death.
   - No book work.
   - Need a fun way of learning.
   - Having teachers help students "understand" material.

question 1 (What is your #1 *personal* concern at Duluth Middle School?) included socialization, friends, relationships, getting along, and racial equality. The topics most frequently mentioned in response to question 2 (What do you feel is most important that you learn next year to help you in the future?) included the need to have good study skills, the need to be computer literate, how to make better decisions, and how to deal with the real world. In response to the third question (If you could change one thing about your academic subjects next year, what would it be?), students wanted to change the amount of book work in classes, the way they learn, and boring classes.

The responses to this survey helped us develop our goals. The responses gave us additional insight into the wants and needs of our students. These responses also helped us in planning our first unit, Human Migration (see Chapter 5). In this unit we focused on a need as identified by the students: the need to know more about themselves.

During that year, we pushed our curriculum toward an authentic, integrative design in which subject area lines dissolved. We rejected the middle school model that suggests every middle school should have the "big four" subject teams, advisory programs, peripheral "exploratory" programs, interest/activities programs, and so on. Instead, we had large blocks of time devoted to a variety of learning experiences (see Chapter 8).

In our quest for coherent curriculum, many things happened. As educators, we questioned ourselves about adolescents, curriculum, and schooling. Our beliefs and educational theories shaped our actions. We had a wonderful year of integrated curriculum. Now, upon reflection, we are reexamining our beliefs and find that they are even more real and more clear as a result of our efforts to integrate the curriculum. We reached our goals and we found that we had gone beyond integrating the curriculum—we had experienced a coherent curriculum.

**Chapter 3**

# COMPONENT: DEMOCRATIC CLASSROOM

It is the middle of January and Ms. Smith's eighth-grade American History class is about to begin their chapter, "The Roots of Democracy in America: The Constitutional Convention of 1787." As she asks the students to open their textbooks, a girl from the back of the class raises her hand and asks, "Why do we have to learn this stuff? What does this have to do with me?" Another student declares, "I'm tired of studying about what happened hundreds of years ago. I want to study about something that is important to me." A chorus of, "Yeah, me too" is echoed around the room.

Ms. Smith sighs and says, "You know why we have to study this. Spring testing is just around the corner, and this will be on the test. Besides, in high school you will need to know all about our democratic government for your Civics class."

The irony of this situation is lost on Ms. Smith.

Democracy in schools is not new. Educators have been teaching about the democratic process through Civics/Government classes for decades. Yet *teaching* about the democratic process is not the same as *experiencing* the democratic process. Learning about democracy and participating in a democracy within the classroom are completely different experiences. Far too many students are in classrooms like Ms. Smith's: they learn about, but are not allowed to participate in, democracy.

To us, a democratic classroom is one in which students and teachers collaborate. It is one in which students' voices are heard and respected. In a democratic classroom, students and teachers might work together in formulating classroom management plans, setting grading policies, or developing curricula. In a democratic classroom, students know they are respected and their input is valued by the teachers and their classmates. Students in this setting are empowered.

A democratic classroom thrives in a safe, risk-taking atmosphere—an atmosphere in which students feel comfortable sharing their thoughts, feelings, and schoolwork. However, to support this "safe" atmosphere, ground rules must be agreed on (e.g., no "put-downs" allowed, and no interrupting speakers allowed). When students know the ground rules will be enforced, they feel more comfortable in expressing their ideas and their feelings. For example, in the year of our quest for coherent curriculum, one of our students stated on a written questionnaire, "I like being able to count on other students. I can see a difference in our classes and the others. It seems that we are more mature."

Student participation is vital to establishing and maintaining a democratic classroom. When students participate in decision making, the context for learning becomes personalized. Learning, then, is based on questions posed by students and teachers working in collaboration. Learning is connected in meaningful ways to the life of the student. Passive learning of an impersonal, fact-driven, fragmented, and disconnected curriculum is replaced by a curriculum that is personal, experiential, integrated, and connected to the world outside the classroom—a curriculum that is coherent. Coherent curriculum requires students to question, examine, and extend their learning. With this curriculum, students must *do* as opposed to just *know*.

Educators know that the most powerful learning takes place when students take an active part in their learning. There is an old Chinese proverb that says:

I hear, and I forget,
I see, and I remember,
I do, and I understand.

Taking this proverb into account, it makes sense, then, to pattern classroom policies on democratic processes so that students have a variety of opportunities to practice the skills necessary to become contributing members of our democratic society.

In this chapter we will share our McHome Team's experiences in setting up and sustaining our democratic classroom: what we did, how we did it, and what we and our students thought about our experiences. Keep in mind that each situation is different and teachers and students need to personalize their efforts for establishing their own democratic classroom.

Developing a democratic classroom, on the McHome Team, incorporated the teaching and modeling of skills and concepts: problem solving, decision making, listening, respecting others, sharing, compromising, discussing, encouraging, questioning respectfully, following directions, explaining, accepting others, being sensitive to others, taking risks, and accepting responsibility. These skills and concepts were integral to developing a safe, risk-taking environment.

## MANAGEMENT PLAN

One way we promoted democracy on the McHome Team was by creating our team management plan in collaboration with our students. Team management plans typically provide guidelines for student conduct. Plans are traditionally created by a single teacher or team of teachers prior to the first day of school without input from students. Generally, at our school, team management plans are posted on the wall for the beginning of school. A typical plan might have a listing of team rules (e.g., students will be respectful of each other, students will come prepared for class, students will stay on task). A typical plan might also include steps taken when students violate rules (e.g., the first infraction will result in a warning, the second infraction will result in a student–teacher conference, the third infraction will result in a phone call home).

We knew we wanted input from our students on our classroom management plan. We also knew that we wanted our classroom management plan to be more than just a behavior management plan. We wanted our plan to help ensure student success. Our administration allowed us to delay posting our plan until the second week of school. We started the process of establishing a democratic classroom by having a McHome Team meeting on the first day of school. Our team meeting began with brainstorming and questioning activities. We wanted our students to tell us why they were in school. We began the conversation by asking, "All of you will be in school for a minimum of 13 years. You began school in kindergarten and will finish 12th grade. If you are to spend all that time in school, what is the point? Just what is the purpose of schooling?" The looks on the faces of our students revealed to us that many of them had never seriously thought about the purpose of schooling.

At first we got the typical answers you would expect from middle school students, such as, "Because there is a law that says we have to be in school" and "Because my parents make me come." These answers were written on the board *without comment.* We did not respond negatively or place judgment on their answers because we were *modeling* for the team the accepting, nonjudgmental behavior that we hoped our students would eventually exhibit. It is this kind of climate that promotes risk taking. We kept probing for further reasons. Finally we began to get more thoughtful responses, such as, "We are in school to be successful in life," "To be prepared for the future," "To get a good education," "To build intelligence," "To help you get a job," "To amount to something we're proud of," "To learn knowledge for life," and "To learn self-discipline."

After discussing the responses, the team came to the conclusion that it would be necessary to be a *good student* to achieve the purpose of schooling. We then asked the students to brainstorm a list of "good student" qualities. They came up with the following:

*A GOOD STUDENT ...*

| | |
|---|---|
| has a positive attitude | is open minded |
| is organized | knows when/where to cut up in class |
| is willing to learn | has good behavior |
| has self-esteem | cooperates |
| is patriotic | listens |
| is trustworthy | is respectful |
| pays attention | stays in school |
| participates | doesn't talk when others are talking |
| tries | does his or her own work |
| has/uses own ideas | is helpful |
| is prepared | does not cheat |
| is responsible | works well with others |
| studies | does not give dirty looks |

We asked the students to look at the list of "good student" characteristics to see if there were similarities. Could we group them into categories in order to get a clearer picture of a "good student"? The students decided that these characteristics seemed to fall into three categories: respect, effort, and responsibility.

Identifying those characteristics that are directly observable was their next task. To help them complete this task, we asked them to think about the following: "Can you always tell if someone is 'paying attention'?" "Could someone who was making eye contact *not* be paying attention?" We asked them to look at the categorized list and identify the characteristics that were unquestionably observable. After taking a few minutes for discussion, we all reviewed the list and then placed an asterisk beside those behaviors which

could be observed. See Figure 3.1 for the characteristics within the three categories and for notations of which ones are observable.

Next, we posed the following questions to the students: "If the purpose of schooling is to prepare students for college, for the job market, or
to be responsible citizens, what should we as teachers do to help you be
successful?" and "What should we do if students are doing those 'observable
behaviors' that are keeping them from being successful?" The students' reac-
tions were varied. One student declared, "I think that you just should talk
to them. Or maybe give them a detention." Another student countered, "I
think you should call home." One even asked, "Why couldn't you just put
them in isolation?" Another student suggested, "I think you should just do
nothing because their grades would fall and that would be their consequence." We reminded them that we wanted to help them be successful in
their schoolwork. We asked them, "What if students are disturbing others
in the class? Is that fair to the others? Don't we have a responsibility to all
of you?"

At this point we had the students get into small groups to discuss a
possible management plan for the team and to identify what we teachers
could do to help *ensure student success* for everyone on our team. After
20 minutes of small-group discussion, each group was ready to share their
ideas with the team. As a team, we discussed the merits of each group's plan,

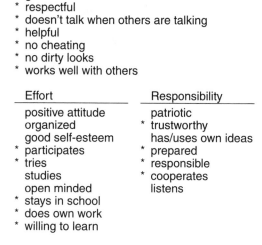

**Figure 3.1.** Three categories of "good student" characteristics.

and with the agreement of everyone (democracy in action), developed the McHome Team Management Plan (see Figure 3.2).

This agreement or consensus is critical for sustaining a democratic classroom. If students who do not agree with the majority feel that their opinions do not matter, then they tend to be unhappy and may undermine decisions made by the majority. When we had students who disagreed with the majority view, we asked them to tell why they felt as they did and what they would be willing to accept in order for the rest of us to gain their support. The benefits of agreement or consensus were twofold. First, students who were in disagreement felt their voices were being heard (which built self-worth and contributed to a more positive attitude), and second, they learned how to negotiate compromise (valuable skills for life).

Our students wanted three warnings recorded in the team management plan before any teacher action occurred. They were concerned that warnings would accumulate too fast if they were consolidated rather than kept separately by each teacher. So it was agreed upon, only after the third warning would a student experience a consequence. See an example of a warning sheet in Figure 3.3.

A student who had earned a fourth warning was separated from the class (placed in another teacher's classroom) to review his warnings and to write a personal plan of improvement. In this plan, the student responded to each of the behaviors that earned him a warning and then devised personal strategies for changing those behaviors. The student's plan of improvement (see Figure 3.4) was attached to his warning sheet and put back into the team management plan notebook. We incorporated this procedure so that students would recognize the relationship between actions, consequences, and accepting responsibility for changing one's own behavior.

The fifth warning resulted in a phone call home. We tried to have the student make this call, if at all possible. This student-placed phone call was extremely helpful in facilitating communication. The student told the par-

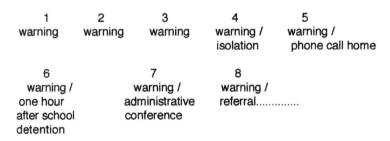

**Figure 3.2.** The McHome Team Management Plan.

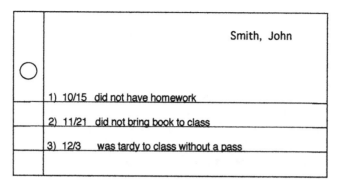

**Figure 3.3.** Example of a student warning sheet.

```
                                              Smith, John

     ◯

     │ 1)  10/15   did not have homework
     │ 2)  11/21   did not bring book to class
     │ 3)  12/3     was tardy to class without a pass
```

**Figure 3.4.** Example of a student plan of improvement.

```
                                              Smith, John

     ◯              Plan of Improvement    12/14
     │ 1) To make sure I won't forget my homework again, I will write my
     │    homework assignments in my assignment calendar and check
     │    before I leave home in the morning to make sure I put my
     │    homework in my bookbag.
     ◯ 2) To make sure I remember to bring my book to class everyday, I
     │    will go to my locker after exploratories and get the books for my
     │    afternoon classes.
```

ent what he had done to earn five warnings, read his personal plan of improvement to his parent, and then told his parent that the next warning would result in a one-hour after-school teacher-issued detention. Our students did not want this phone-home step. This was an ideal opportunity to let them know that in a democratic classroom the teachers also have a voice. We explained that if they went from warning number four to a detention, without a phone call home, their parents (and our administrator) would be upset. We let them know we were not willing to have this happen. We told them our job was to keep their parents informed. Now, if they did not want their parents called, then it was their responsibility to *not* receive that fifth warning. This was an explanation that they understood and could live with. Explaining our reasons to them instead of telling them it would be this way "because we said so" was also modeling democratic behavior. Our students needed to know that we were willing to take the time to explain.

When the sixth warning was earned we would fill out a detention form and give it to the student; the student would take it home, have a parent or guardian sign it, and then return the form to school on or before the day of detention. Under no circumstances was a student allowed to serve detention without a parent-signed form (see Figure 3.5), because in the past, students had told their parents they were staying for after-school help and did not tell them they were staying for detention.

The seventh warning resulted in a student *conference* with one of our administrators. We attached a copy of the student's warning sheet and plan of improvement to the conference form. Our administrator liked this idea because it gave her the opportunity to talk with the student before she assigned additional consequences. Students are frequently sent to administrators for disciplinary action without that administrator previously having

---

Monday, December 5
date


John Smith
name of student

Dear  Mr. and Mrs. Smith

Your son/daughter will be staying for detention on (day) Wed.
( date) Dec. 7 from  2:20  to    3:20   the reason for the detention is:
   John has received his sixth warning for being unprepared for class
 on Monday, December 5. According to our team management plan
John will serve a one-hour-after-school detention.  Please sign this
form and have John return it to me tomorrow.

---

Elaine Homestead
teacher signature


**Student may not serve detention without this form signed.**
If you have any questions please feel free to call me at 476-3372.

I agree to have my child serve detention on the above date. I
understand that I am responsible for transportation home from school
after the detention.

_____          _____
        parent signature                          date

**Figure 3.5.** Example of a student detention form.

seen the student. The administrator's first inclination is to counsel the student before assigning a punishment. Usually, this lack of a consequence is viewed as being nonsupportive in the eyes of the beleaguered (and often angry) teacher. It is especially frustrating when the student comes back to the class and tells the other students that "nothing" was done. Putting this "conference" step in our plan worked well for all involved. The student had a chance to talk with the administrator about previous behaviors without fear of punishment, the administrator had the opportunity to give the student a chance to explain past behaviors, and together they had an opportunity to plan an appropriate course of action to *help the student be successful.* The administrative conference was documented (on a school conference form) and filed in the McHome Team management book. As a result of this conference, there was complete understanding between administrator, student, and teacher on what would occur if the student earned another warning.

The eighth warning (and all subsequent warnings in a grading period) resulted in an administrative referral. At this step, our administrator assigned a consequence. This could be an administrative detention for 2 or 4 hours after school, a day of in-school suspension (the student would be separated from the rest of the school and supervised by an adult in a separate "in-school" room), or Saturday school (an 8:00–12:00 detention).

The "slate was wiped clean" for each student at the beginning of each new grading period. At the beginning of every grading period (6 weeks), each student gave us a blank sheet of notebook paper with their name in the upper right-hand corner. We alphabetized them and put them into our three-ring McHome Team management notebook. Each time a student earned a warning, we recorded it on their sheet until the end of the grading period when we started all over again.

On paper, our behavior management plan may not have looked much different from typical classroom management plans. The difference was that students and teachers codeveloped the plan rather than teachers imposing a plan on students. Student ownership of the plan made all the difference in the world in their acceptance of consequences. Our students understood that the management plan was developed to *help them be successful.* As one student remarked, "Your teachers aren't working against you, they are working for you." Although students still didn't like it when a warning was issued, each grumbled less because there was genuine ownership of the behavior management plan.

## GROUP PROCESSING

An indispensable element of the democratic classroom is group processing. Group processing involves reflecting (orally or in writing) on group actions to determine what is helpful or unhelpful and then making group decisions on what to keep or change. One way we used group processing was by getting together as a team (all 58 students) to reflect upon and talk about various issues affecting us.

At one of our first team meetings, we collaborated on the establishment of group norms (what behaviors were and were not acceptable). We wrote our team decisions on chart paper and taped them to the wall. We modeled for our students how to conduct lively, but controlled, discussions. After this team meeting, students took turns conducting subsequent team meetings. The agreed-upon norms were:

> We will raise our hands and wait to be recognized before talking.
> We will listen to each other with respect.
> No put-downs allowed.
> Anyone not able to follow these guidelines will be asked to leave the
>     room for five minutes.

During student-conducted team meetings, a greater sense of ownership in the decisions that were made was evident. For example, our students often designed their own rubrics (see Chapter 4) that were used to grade processes, products, and performances. In response to a written question, "How do you feel about using rubrics for assessment as opposed to traditional multiple-choice, fill-in-the-blank, true/false tests, etc?" a student candidly responded, "I like true/false tests better, but I guess that's because it's easier and taking a free ride, but I learn more skills, like following through with what you say you're gonna do, with a rubric." This example of student ownership of decisions was vital to the democratic process because it motivated students to take responsibility for their decisions and actions.

## GRADING POLICY

Educators know that, for the most part, good grades are often the result of effort and are not solely intelligence based. Because our integrated curriculum was challenging, we wanted our students to realize that they could succeed through effort. We wanted each of them to experience the self-satisfaction that comes from being successful by working hard. During the first 6 weeks, the grading policy was teacher imposed and not developed "democratically" with our students. We did this so the students could experience success as a result of their efforts. The criteria for the first 6 weeks' grading policy were:

A grade less than 92 (our school district's A) is a *mandatory* redo.

Warnings will be given to students that do not redo their assignments.

Redo work must be turned in the next school day, in homeroom (7:30).

Incomplete work is not acceptable. Complete the work and take a late grade.

Late work will be accepted, *if* it is complete, at –5 points per day. After 3 days, work will not be accepted and will result in a grade of zero.

Needless to say, the first 6 weeks many of our students accumulated six warnings or more. Several students stayed for an after-school detention. A few students even reached warning number eight, which earned them an administrative referral. Because we had our administrator's support, the "get tough" policy worked for the first grading period. Surprisingly, our students' parents were very supportive of our efforts. They expressed thanks for our efforts in making their children work hard. At the end of the first grading period, 38 from our team of students made the honor roll! The students were astonished. Many of them had never been on the honor roll before. Our point had been made. In the minds of our students, effort and grades had been indelibly linked.

Our first "end of the grading period" team meeting (group processing) activity was again lively. We needn't have worried about student input. They couldn't wait to have their say. The first order of business was to discuss the grading policy. Each and every student on the team had strong feelings about it. As a team, we discussed what was good about the policy, what students wanted changed, and why. Students liked the idea of being able to redo their work. What they did not like was being *made* to redo it. One student argued, quite sensibly, "You say you want us to be responsible. But if you want us to be responsible, then you need to let us make some of our own decisions." It was hard to argue with reasoning like that. Every student wanted to decide whether or not to redo the work. Quite a few stated there was nothing wrong with a "B." We cautioned the students that deciding not to redo an assignment could result in the natural consequences of poor grades and angry parents. Students agreed that assuming that responsibility was their job and not ours. Hearing our students asking for the opportunity to accept responsibility for their own actions was sweet music indeed!

The students decided that incomplete work should not be accepted. However, they did not like the idea of a classmate who turned in late work being given the opportunity to redo it. Students felt it was unfair for someone who turned in their work late to be able to redo the assignment (for a possible 100), just like someone who worked hard to get their work completed and turned in on time. Their rationale was that if someone took an extra day to complete an assignment, their work should be correct, and it therefore should not need to be redone. The whole team agreed to change this part of the grading policy.

After listening to their concerns, we voiced one of our own. We noticed that a few students were using the redo policy in an inappropriate way. These students were using us as editors for their papers. They were handing in poor-quality work, and then, after we had identified their errors, were redoing their papers. We told the team that we were very uncomfortable with this. It made us feel as though we were fostering academic irresponsibility. We stressed that we wanted them to turn in their very best efforts for grading, and then, if they did not do well, we would reteach and they would be given the opportunity to rework their assignments. They agreed.

Modeling the democratic process, we compromised with our students. This compromise led to the following grading policy changes: Mistakes made due to lack of understanding would be allowed to be redone, but mistakes due to carelessness would not. The –5 points per day for late work was acceptable to all. Students did not have a problem with a zero grade, after being given the opportunity to turn in work late for up to 3 days. We wrote all suggestions on chart paper and the team came to a consensus on the grading policy for the second 6-week grading period. Even though it could have been revised at any time, the team opted to keep this policy for the remainder of the year:

Students may *choose* to redo assignments if errors are *not* due to carelessness.

No warnings for not redoing assignments. The grade will be the natural consequence.

Redo work must be turned in the next school day in homeroom (7:30).

Incomplete work is not acceptable. Complete the work and take a late grade.

Late work cannot be redone.

Late work is accepted *if* it is complete at –5 points per day. After 3 days, work will not be accepted and will result in a grade of zero.

It is interesting to note that the number of our students making the honor roll dropped from 38 to 19 the second grading period. This was a direct result of our students making their own decisions regarding the redo policy. The important lesson learned was that each student took responsibility for the grades he or she earned.

## GROUP-WORK GUIDELINES

Having our students help to develop group-work guidelines was another way to have them experience democracy within our classroom. Establishing and adhering to group guidelines was essential to the McHome Team's success because much of our class time involved working in groups. We began the process by having the team divide into four-member groups. We gave them an activity to do *without* any teacher direction. We had previously notified the teachers on our hall to expect noise and asked for their forbearance for a little while. One activity sheet per group was handed out, then we stepped back and observed.

At the end of about 15 minutes, we stopped the activity. Now was a crucial time to evaluate the learning environment. Students were excited at this point and were ready to discuss such questions as, "How well did your group complete the task?" "What did you notice about the noise level of the group?" and "of the classroom?" "What did your group members do during the work time?" "How did your group set up for the completion of the task?" "Did you finish?" "Why or why not?" These questions led to a team discussion regarding the need for group-work guidelines.

We asked each group to brainstorm guidelines they felt were necessary for establishing a productive learning environment. Groups shared their ideas with the team and we compiled a team list. Examples of their suggestions for making group work productive included no put-downs, stay with your group, talk softly to your group only, and everyone do their fair share. From the team list, the students then decided on the most important group-work guidelines to incorporate into team policy:

Cooperate (try; respect ideas; listen; positive attitude).
Stay on task (group project assignment only).
Stay with your group.

We advised the team to limit the number of guidelines to the most important four items because long lists are often formidable and students tend to ignore them. Calling our policy "guidelines" rather than "rules" was an important psychological distinction. We intentionally made this distinction because most middle schoolers have an aversion to "rules," even ones they make for themselves.

## CONCLUSION

Collaborating with students on the team management plan, grading policy, and group-work guidelines helped lay the foundation for a democratic classroom. As the year progressed, our students had further opportunities for input. They collaborated with us on curriculum development beginning with the very first unit. Students were given choices of assignments and choices of evaluation methods. By the end of the year, they were able to develop their own unit with *us* working as consultants and guides rather than as directors of their learning (see Chapter 5).

Sustaining a democratic classroom is sometimes messy, often loud, and always takes time. Anyone who has ever watched the U.S. Senate or House of Representatives debate or news clips of Britain's House of Commons knows that this is so. Students, however, are frequently impatient with democratic processes. Several of our students expressed their displeasure when we asked them to respond in writing, at the end of the first 6 weeks, regarding our democratic classroom: "I didn't like how it took a long, long time for us to decide on something. It took forever to vote on something." "There was too much arguing and fussing." "I don't like having to vote and make plans for almost everything we do." Teachers and students need to be aware of, and should frequently discuss, the challenges inherent in maintaining a democratic classroom.

A vital part of a democratic classroom is the teacher knowing how each and every student feels about what is happening on the team. The outgoing student will make sure her voice is heard. It is important for students who are not inclined to speak up to be heard as well. Teachers can make sure that each student has input by having team meetings, small-group discussions, one-on-one discussions with the students, or by asking students to respond in writing to specific questions or concerns. Often students who are shy will have no trouble putting their thoughts in writing when they would not dream of speaking up in front of the team.

Sometimes teachers may not even know that students are experiencing a problem. For example, after the first grading period, we had our students respond in writing to this question: "What do you like the least about our democratic classroom?" The following are similar thoughts expressed by three students who had not been very vocal up to that point:

- The majority always rules. For an example, when picking due dates, some people needed more time to work on their project, but the deadline was shortened so our group had to rush through our project. And when it was time to present, I felt that our presentation could have been made better. If we had more time.
- Somebody ends up unhappy when we vote. Some people, even

though they are peers, tend to take over our classroom. Some people's opinions matter more.

- Sometimes some kids don't get to do things they want to do, so they have to do what the class wants.

Having students put their ideas and concerns in writing helped us address these issues. At team meetings, we discussed the issues that were troubling some members of the team. It was in these team meetings that our students really experienced the give and take of the democratic classroom. Students came to understand that if they didn't speak up, then they had to accept the decisions that were made without their input. Our team was functioning as a democracy.

Because we collaborated with our students on team decisions, personal ownership of the learning process took place, which accomplished many things. First, it promoted positive attitudes toward school. Students were contributing members of the team and, therefore, felt a vital part of the team. As one student declared, "I personally liked being able to pick my own topic. The reason for this is because I was more involved in what I was doing, instead of being bored with regular old book work, that the teacher assigns."

Second, personal ownership helped facilitate student–teacher communication. Students were listened to and were encouraged to participate in classroom decision making. Several students voiced their appreciation when they said, "I really like being able to make our own decisions and being able to talk it out." "The class was sort of fun. We made our own due dates, rubrics, and assignments. Not like the last 7 years of 'teacher rules class.'" "I like the democratic classroom because we get to take part in decisions and contribute ideas."

Third, personal ownership increased learning. Students' learning improves when they are studying what is important and relevant to them. Our students did well not only the first grading period but for the rest of the year.

Fourth, personal ownership improved classroom discipline because "interested" students are far less likely to be disruptive. On one of her school visits during the second grading period, Elizabeth interviewed four students who were working together on their project presentation. She asked them about discipline problems. It got very quiet. The students looked at each other, then at Elizabeth. After a couple of minutes, one of them said, "I never thought about it, but we don't have discipline problems on our team." At the end of the day, when Elizabeth shared this with us, we reacted just as the students had. We hadn't thought about it either, but we really didn't have any discipline problems.

It is worth noting here that a democratic classroom is *not* a classroom where students *rule*. Teachers are professionals and are responsible to students, parents, and administrators. A democratic classroom is one in which students and their teachers collaborate. But collaboration is not easy, because a lot of the authority is taken away from the teacher—and that can be scary. Keeping the lines of communication open (being comfortable in expressing ideas and feelings for both teachers and students) is the key to successful collaboration.

It is important to recognize that once student input is elicited, teachers cannot go back to an autocratic classroom again. Once students find a voice in the classroom, they demand to be heard. Once teachers experience the enthusiasm their students have for the democratic classroom, they will not want to go back to making all the decisions.

When asked what they liked about our democratic classroom, some students responded:

- I really liked the freedom. We really got a lot of skills out of it by structuring our time and plans. I also liked the way we can discuss our own opinions and views on the way we see things. I really felt that we all made a difference.
- I like being able to give my input on whether or not we get to do something. I also like working with other people besides our friends. I think all of us need to branch out and get to know others.
- I enjoyed having this kind of class. The teachers didn't tell us what to do. I liked that! I think it becomes more interesting like that.
- The thing I like most about it is that we make the decisions that affect us.

Implementing a democratic classroom empowered our students. In our democratic classroom, our students exhibited more self-confidence, higher self-esteem, and were more willing to take intellectual risks than students of previous years.

Why should we have democratic classrooms? James Beane advises that, "We should have democratic classrooms, quite simply, because we live in a democracy" (Vars & Beane, 1994).

# Chapter 4

# COMPONENT: TRADITIONAL AND ALTERNATIVE ASSESSMENT

Preparing students for "life roles" (e.g., worker, citizen, family member, life-long learner) outside of school is a primary function of schooling today. In preparation for these life roles, students must learn to solve complex tasks, communicate clearly and logically, think critically, become self-directed learners, and work effectively with a diversity of people.

For students to attain these skills and attitudes, they need multiple opportunities to work together with their teachers "doing" schoolwork that is authentic (i.e., more like the world outside of the classroom), personally meaningful to students (i.e., helps young people understand themselves and their world), and rigorous (i.e., mentally challenging). The curriculum should be organized around the real problems of personal and social concern to students (Beane, 1990). An important component of this curriculum is the utilization of knowledge and skills from the various disciplines (Beane, 1995a). In this curriculum, students take an active part: they work with their teachers to develop, test, revise, evaluate, and implement their plans.

Middle schoolers are at various levels of development (Toepfer, 1992b). The physical development of these young people varies from the childlike prepubescent to the adultlike adolescent (Tanner, 1972). The social and emotional development of middle schoolers varies as well. They can act childish one moment and make mature decisions the next. The cognitive development of middle schoolers varies just as widely, from the concrete to the abstract and back again to the concrete (Dana & Tippins, 1993).

In addition to students' developmental differences, there are also differences in students' learning styles. Some students learn better when they read (visual learners), some when they listen (auditory learners), some when they touch (tactile learners), some when they are physically active (kinesthetic learners), and some students utilize a combination of learning styles.

In addition to having differing learning styles, Gardner (1993) maintained that humans have a broad range of abilities or intelligences. He grouped these intelligences into the seven categories of linguistic, logical-mathematical, spatial, bodily-kinesthetic, musical, interpersonal, and intrapersonal. Armstrong (1994) advised educators to take into account students' differing intelligences when developing the curriculum because students in our classrooms are a kaleidoscope of developmental levels, learning styles, and intelligences.

Incorporating a variety of classroom assessments (a variety of traditional assessments and also a variety of alternative assessments) provides a clearer "picture" of what it is that students know and can do. A variety of assessments provides for student differences: differing learning styles, differing academic strengths and weaknesses, and differing intelligences that are evident in every classroom.

Traditional classroom assessments such as worksheets, true/false, fill-in-the-blank, and multiple-choice tests are, well, "traditional." They are familiar to students, teachers, and parents. Traditional assessments are easy to design, administer, and score. They are usually designed to elicit lower-order thinking (student recall of factual information). They are not, however, designed to evaluate students' demonstrations of complex tasks.

What gets included in traditional classroom assessments is representative of what the teacher thinks is important to know and may not necessarily be representative of what the student knows or does not know. Students often prepare for traditional classroom assessments by playing a "guessing game" of what may or may not be on the assessment. After the "test," students have difficulty remembering what they learned. Students who consistently do well on traditional classroom assessments often possess verbal and quantitative strengths. Students who are strong in other areas (e.g., creativity, music, art) do not have many opportunities to show their strengths on traditional assessments.

Alternative assessments such as multimedia presentations, computer-generated presentations, debates, models, and simulations allow students opportunities to demonstrate complex tasks in a variety of ways. Developing alternative assessments should be a collaborative effort between students and teachers. It is through this process of collaboration that clarity in expectations and a consensus of purpose emerges for both students and teachers. Determining how to evaluate and then derive grades from these authentic learning tasks should also be a collaborative effort. Collaboration on the evaluation of student performance is essential because it is during the evaluation design process that the criteria for student success are clearly defined for students and teachers.

Changing the McHome Team's instructional program from a traditional separate-subject content-driven curriculum (i.e., a focus on facts and concepts) to an integrated student-centered curriculum (i.e., one that connects all aspects of the curriculum—the working world, subject content and skills, and social skills—for students and teachers [Pate, Homestead, and McGinnis, 1995]) required us to make significant changes in instructional strategies, in planned activities, and in how we evaluated our students. Prior to our quest for coherent curriculum, we had focused on instructional strategies such as lecture and discussion and classroom activities such as worksheets and peer tutoring that we thought would help our students learn subject-specific facts and skills. We attempted to determine how much "factual knowledge" our students remembered by administering traditional classroom assessments.

In our quest for coherent curriculum, the scope and sequences, textbooks, and separate-subject curriculum guides would not be the central organizers for our units of study. We were determined to put the needs and concerns of our students first. Our aim was to develop *with our students* units of study that were personally meaningful, mentally challenging, and connected as much as possible to the world outside of the classroom (i.e., authentic). We wanted to help prepare our students for a changing and increasingly challenging world.

To illustrate how assessment was integrated into our student-teacher cocreated curriculum we provide an explanation of our curriculum design process.

## CURRICULUM DESIGN PROCESS

In designing this more complex and demanding integrated curriculum, we incorporated the unit/lesson design format developed in 1992 by our school system, Gwinnett County Public Schools. This sequentially formulated step-by-step process provided for the *planned* inclusion of thinking skills, problem-solving skills, and social and affective skills. This design process also provided for student demonstration of those skills (i.e., the performance assessment).

This curriculum design process was called "designing down" because the sequence for *designing* our curriculum was in one direction: The steps were as follows:

Theme identification → Determining the focus questions → Linking skills to content → Developing the performance assessment → Planning the learning activities → Searching for resources to support the learning activities

See Figure 4.1 for an example of how this process was used in planning for a specific topic. The sequence for *implementing* our curriculum, however, was in the opposite direction: We began with collecting our resources, which were utilized in the learning activities, which in turn taught our students what they needed to know and be able to do for their performance assessment, which was designed to demonstrate their knowledge and skills.

| Content Focus Question | What are historical and current examples of events that fulfill/deny basic H/CR and what were the effects upon society? |
|---|---|
| Linking Skills to Content | 1. Integrate effective information-gathering techniques to apply knowledge of historic and current attempts that fulfill/deny basic H/CR and how these attempts affected society.<br>2. Orally and non-verbally communicate historical and current examples of events that fulfill/deny basic H/CR and the effects upon society. |
| Performance Assessment | LIVING HISTORY TIMELINE:<br>Through a skit students will give an accurate and complete account of a H/CR event and its effect upon society. |
| Learning Activities | The McHome Team Rights and Responsibilities [group activity]<br>Founding of the first colony/Salem Witch Trials [discussion]<br>Industrial Revolution [timeline, video, lecture] Slave System [readings]<br>Road to Am. Revolution [Paul Revere's Ride, lecture, activity, Roots Unit]<br>Bill of Rights [activity packet] Indian Removal/Trail of Tears [Jigsaw activity]<br>Pre-Civil War Conditions [worksheets, data retrieval chart, class discussions]<br>Dred Scott Decision [simulation]<br>Reconstruction [worksheets/group presentations]<br>Holocaust [B'nai B'rith gallery of photos/discussion]<br>Civil Rights Movement [timeliner/discussion/movie] New Hate Groups [article]<br>The Georgia Flag Flap: A Flag for All Georgians   Scriptwriting<br>Vietnam Era [lecture/notetaking]<br>Balkan Crisis [data retrieval chart/advance organizer/timeline/peace conf.] |
| Resources | GA in Am. Society          The Write Source 2000          GA History Book<br>The American Centuries   America! America!                    Redbook<br>B'nai B'rith                       Prentice Hall Literature Silver   Timeliner<br>The Atlanta Constitution   "The Industrial Revolution"        "Roots" |

**Figure 4.1.** Example of a design down unit plan.

*Step 1.* The first step in the design process was to determine the topic or theme for study, for example, Human and Civil Rights and Responsibilities. At the beginning of the year, themes were organized around our school system's newly restructured social studies curriculum. Our students accepted more responsibility for theme determination and curriculum development as they gained experience.

*Step 2.* After deciding on a theme for study, the next step was to formulate focus questions to research and explore. Our students were connected to the theme, right from the start, by the initial focus question. For example, in our unit Human and Civil Rights and Responsibilities, the first question we explored was, "What evidence exists that teenagers have rights?" The next question to explore was, "What are historical and current examples of events that fulfill/deny basic H/CR and what were the effects upon society?"

*Step 3.* Once the focus questions were determined, the higher-order thinking, problem-solving, and social and affective skills that would be incorporated in the unit were identified. This decision was based on overall student needs as determined by us (teachers and students) working together. Did our students need practice in utilizing a variety of resources to answer the focus question? Did our students need practice in synthesizing the information gathered so they could apply their knowledge and skills? Which social skills (such as active listening, taking turns, encouraging participation, sharing materials, and reaching consensus) did our students need to focus on? Which communication skills (such as writing to communicate feelings, speaking effectively in front of a group, and preparing and delivering a persuasive argument) would they demonstrate?

*Step 4.* The next step in the unit design process, following the identification of skills, was to design the performance assessment. The performance assessment required our students to *demonstrate* the thinking, problem-solving, and social and affective skills and knowledge gained during the course of the project. For example, they could decide to design a simulation, write a play, make a model, or organize a debate.

For this particular unit, our students wanted to "do something big." They decided to create a "Living History Timeline." The students identified 11 issues and events to reenact, ranging from the Salem Witch Trials to the conflict in the former Yugoslavia. They wrote scripts, designed backdrops, and created costumes.

*Step 5.* The next step in the unit design process was to plan the learning activities. The learning activities were developed to do two things at one time: help students gain the knowledge and practice the skills they must demonstrate in the performance assessment.

*Step 6.* The final step in the design process was to locate appropriate resources. For our project-based integrated curriculum, a wide variety of resources was necessary. Students utilized their textbooks and resources in our school's media center, wrote away for information, invited guest speakers, conducted interviews in person and over the phone, used an on-line computer service, and made off-campus fact-finding trips.

This method of unit/lesson design provided for purposeful incorporation of higher-order thinking skills (incorporation of higher-order thinking skills was not left to chance), provided focus and a plan for learning for students and teachers, and provided a framework for developing appropriate assessments at the beginning of the unit or lesson.

At the beginning of the school year, because this way of teaching and learning was new for our students, we modeled this design process. We explained how decisions are made regarding the topic (or theme) for study. We intentionally connected the theme to the interests of our students. We demonstrated how to connect the focus questions and skills in order to develop the performance assessment. We also constantly reminded our students how we were extending our resources beyond our textbooks.

Over time, our students began to understand how this design process worked and why we were using it. Educators know that active participation results in greater learning gains than passive uninvolvement. So, to help our students fully understand and utilize the process, we had them prepare lessons for the team. The unit we were working on was Human Interactions and the Environment. In this unit, students chose environmental issues of personal concern to investigate (see Chapter 5). In the course of their investigations students identified science concepts they needed to learn (and teach others on the team) in order to fully understand their environmental issue. For example, one group of students, concerned about the thinning of the ozone layer, determined that to fully understand this issue they (and our team) needed to know what ozone is, how ozone is made and destroyed, what the purpose of the ozone layer is, and where the ozone layer is located. Groups worked together to plan their "mini-lessons." Each group had to determine what their "students" needed to know, what skills these "students" would practice in gaining that knowledge, how the "students" were to demonstrate their knowledge, what learning activities would be appropriate to gain the knowledge, and what resources would be needed to support the learning (see Figure 4.2).

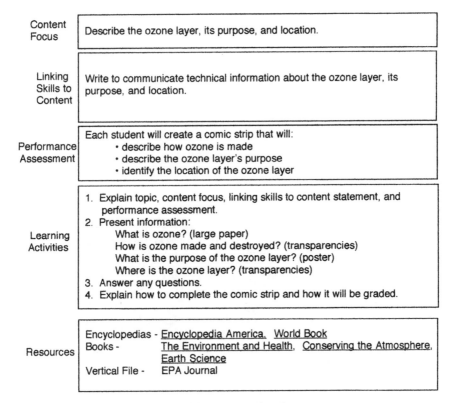

| Content Focus | Describe the ozone layer, its purpose, and location. |
|---|---|
| Linking Skills to Content | Write to communicate technical information about the ozone layer, its purpose, and location. |
| Performance Assessment | Each student will create a comic strip that will:<br>• describe how ozone is made<br>• describe the ozone layer's purpose<br>• identify the location of the ozone layer |
| Learning Activities | 1. Explain topic, content focus, linking skills to content statement, and performance assessment.<br>2. Present information:<br>    What is ozone? (large paper)<br>    How is ozone made and destroyed? (transparencies)<br>    What is the purpose of the ozone layer? (poster)<br>    Where is the ozone layer? (transparencies)<br>3. Answer any questions.<br>4. Explain how to complete the comic strip and how it will be graded. |
| Resources | Encyclopedias - <u>Encyclopedia America, World Book</u><br>Books -     <u>The Environment and Health, Conserving the Atmosphere, Earth Science</u><br>Vertical File -   EPA Journal |

**Figure 4.2.** A lesson plan developed by a group of students.

After each group had taught their mini-lesson we checked their understanding of and feelings about the lesson design process by asking each to reflect in writing. As one of our students put it:

A designing down form is a form that helps the teachers explain what they are going to teach and what and how they are going to teach it. My group used it to show what we were going to teach in our mini-lesson. Our mini-lesson was very clear after we finished our designing down form. We wrote down everything we were going to do and we did it. On the designing down form are a list of boxes in a certain order. I think that they are in a logical order so that I don't get confused with what I'm doing. This is brand new to me so it was like a gift when they put the boxes in this order. This was a good idea, because it gave me a crystal-clear idea of what I'm doing.

## RUBRICS

To evaluate student performance, we collaboratively created rubrics. Elsewhere (Pate, Homestead, & McGinnis, 1993) we have defined a rubric as a scaled set of criteria that clearly defines for the student and teacher what a range of acceptable and unacceptable performances look like.

Each rubric described the criteria for each level of performance, from poor to excellent. The rubric not only permitted an evaluation of the students' performance, it also became a guide for planning their work (see Figure 4.3). Therefore, the rubric was developed *before* our students began working on their projects.

In the article on rubrics, we stated:

> Rubrics should have such detail that no one (students, teachers, parents) has questions as to how well the activity was done. The following are general guidelines for developing rubrics:
>
> 1. Make a list of the most important part of a learning activity. Use this list to develop rubric sections, which can include process, content, mechanics, presentation, source variety, neatness, and so on.
> 2. Develop a scale for each section showing expected criteria. Start with what "Excellence" or an "A" looks like. Scale down for as many additional categories as you require. Each section may have a different number of criteria assigned to it.
> 3. Weight the rubric sections. Determine what sections are most important and weight those accordingly. For example, in the presentation rubric the sections on eye contact, posture, and voice projection were all weighted the same. However, organization was determined to be the most important part of the presentation and was weighted more. Visual aids and presentation length were not considered as important and were weighted less. (p. 27)

Cocreating the rubric helped our students develop the ability to recognize and set high standards for themselves and evaluate their own work. Having students participate in rubric design also helped to take the uncertainty out of grading. In response to the question, "What is a rubric used for?" one student commented that rubrics let students "know ahead of time what and how everything is graded. It's a fair way, so neither side (teacher/student) can argue about the grade."

As students became more comfortable using the unit/lesson design process and developing rubrics, they eventually designed their own projects and rubrics. During our Human Interactions unit students selected topics of personal concern, determined appropriate skills to work on, designed alternative assessments, and created rubrics. One group of four young women were concerned about the hungry people in Somalia and were

# Multi-Media Presentation Rubric
### A McHome Team Creation

Name: _____

<u>Eye Contact with Audience</u>

| | | | Item x Weight | Item Total |
|---|---|---|---|---|
| 1<br>rarely | 2<br>not often | 3<br>often | ___ x _6_ = | _____ |

<u>Posture</u>

| | | | | |
|---|---|---|---|---|
| 1<br>often - slouches; sways; often turns back on audience; fidgets | 2<br>sometimes - slouches; sways; turns back on audience; fidgets | 3<br>stands straight; faces audience; movements appropriate to presentation | ___ x _6_ = | _____ |

<u>Voice Projection</u>

| | | | | |
|---|---|---|---|---|
| 1<br>words not pronounced clearly and volume too low | 2<br>words not pronounced clearly or volume too low | 3<br>words pronounced and heard clearly | ___ x _6_ = | _____ |

<u>Organization</u>

| | | | | |
|---|---|---|---|---|
| 1<br>information not presented in a logical interesting sequence; the audience could not follow | 2<br>information was interesting but not presented in a logical order | 3<br>information presented in a logical, interesting sequence which the audience could follow | ___ x _7_ = | _____ |

<u>Visual Aid</u>

| | | | | |
|---|---|---|---|---|
| 1<br>two different types of media; visual aid not relevant to outcomes/content; messy; minimal artistic effort | 2<br>two different types of media; visual aid relevant to outcomes/content; neat; adequate artistic effort | 3<br>more than two different types of media; visual aid relevant to outcomes/content; very neat; excellent artistic effort | ___ x _5_ = | _____ |

<u>Time</u>

| | | | | |
|---|---|---|---|---|
| 1<br>less than 10 minutes | 2<br>10 to 14 minutes | 3<br>at least 15 minutes | ___ x _3_ = | _____ |

BONUS POINT(1) ___                    **TOTAL**_____

**Figure 4.3.** A team-developed rubric for presentations.

| Content Focus | How are the starving people of Somalia affecting my world and how can I make a difference? |
|---|---|
| Linking Skills to Content | We will recognize problems of how hunger is affecting our world and make a difference by recognizing opportunities to help. We will devise, implement, evaluate, and revise a plan of action to help the hungry. We will also select and engage in service activities that help the hungry for the mutual benefit of self, family, community. |
| Performance Assessment | We will present the class our project through posters, a video tape, and a slide show. We will make a difference by asking classes to donate money. We will send the money to the CARE Foundation. We will in return buy food for the starving people in Somalia. |

| Learning Activities | Activities | Skills |
|---|---|---|
| | •write letters to CARE, and write to homeroom teachers explaining our project | •letter writing, gathering information, cooperate effectively with a diversity of people, select and read a variety of information to communicate |
| | •collect money from homeroom teachers | •use mathematics to count and add the money |
| | •talk to each homeroom class about our project | •public-speaking skills, manners, and patience |
| | •use SIRS | •data collection, use technology to collect information |
| | •schedule time in a meaningful way | •organization, thinking, listening, and speaking skills |
| | •write a rubric and step-by-step plan | •writing, thinking, listening, and organization skills |
| | •called CARE and collected information that was not in the information they sent | •manners in the phone |

| Resources | CARE Foundation, Time Magazine, National Geographic, SIRS |
|---|---|

**Figure 4.4.** Project plan developed by a group of four students.

determined to make a difference. They developed their project plan as in Figure 4.4. To evaluate their performance assessment and help direct their project work (which was a money-collection project and a group presentation to our team) they created a rubric (see Figure 4.5).

## ASSESSMENT EXAMPLES

Assessing the McHome Team students involved determining what we wanted our students to know. Depending on the theme we were studying, this would be information from our textbooks (subject-area content) as well as information from outside-of-school resources.

| Actions | Not 1 | Not Quite 2 | Good 3 | Perfect 4 | Comments |
|---|---|---|---|---|---|
| State the causes of the hunger problem and how hunger is affecting Somalia. | having 1 fact on the causes of why there is hunger in Somalia | having 2 facts on the causes of why there is hunger in Somalia | having 3 facts on the causes of why there is hunger in Somalia but not how they affect the people of Somalia | having 3 facts on the causes of why there is hunger in Somalia and how they're affecting Somalia in neat, final form | |
| To make a difference we will devise a plan to help the hungry. | having 3 or less step-by-step plan statements | write a step-by-step plan having 4 step-by-step plan statements | write a step-by-step plan to help with at least 5 plan statements | write a step-by-step plan with at least 6 or more plan statements | |
| We will implement a plan to help the hungry in Somalia. | create a letter but not enough copies for each homeroom | create a letter, rough draft, and only explain letter | create a letter for every teacher, rough draft | create a letter for every homeroom and explain the letter and project Spare-A-Lunch | |
| We will evaluate a plan to help the hungry in Somalia. | a written essay on only what went wrong | a written essay on own project in rough draft form | a written essay on our project on Somalia mentioning what went wrong and right, rough draft | write an essay with proper mechanics in final form on what went wrong and right with our project on the hungry in Somalia | |
| We will revise a plan to help the hungry in Somalia, orally and as a group | video tape of conversation, but only one minute in the conversation | video tape of the conversation and only 3 minutes in the conversation | video tape of the conversation and only 4 minutes long | video tape of the conversation and 5 or more minutes long | |

**Figure 4.5.** Rubric for project plan. Rubric: hunger for Somalia project.

Assessing our students also involved determining what we wanted our students to be able to do. This involved identifying the skills they would practice and demonstrate during their project (the process) as well as at the end of their project (the product). It is important to understand that our students demonstrated the skills (i.e., what we wanted them to be able to do) *by way of* the information (i.e., what we wanted them to know). The skills were *not* learned or demonstrated in isolation from the information or subject-area content. Once these determinations were made, we codeveloped the appropriate assessments.

Content (subject-area) information was evaluated using traditional as well as alternative methods of assessment. For example, in the Human and Civil Rights and Responsibilities unit students were given multiple-choice, true-false, and fill-in-the-blank tests as well as worksheets to check their understanding of historical information that was relevant to the theme: founding of the first colony, Salem Witch Trials, events leading to the American Revolution, the Bill of Rights, the history of slavery in America, Indian Removal and the Trail of Tears, events and issues leading to the Civil War, Reconstruction, the Holocaust, the Civil Rights Movement, the Vietnam War and the protest movement, new hate groups, and war in the former Yugoslavia. The students also demonstrated their understanding of these events through alternative assessments: a simulation of the Dred Scott trial, Jigsaw activities, oral presentations, journal writings, developing Colonial-era "broadsides," discussions, timelines, and data retrieval charts. Many times the assessment and the learning activity were one and the same. For example, as each group of students presented their information to the class regarding Indian Removal and the Trail of Tears, it was both a learning activity (Jigsaw) and an assessment (oral group presentation/performance).

All too often, our students wanted to skip right to the fun part of project work (which involved making a product of some kind such as a mural, model, or skit) and would overlook the most important part of the project, which was the process. So we developed assessments for the process part of project work with our students. We created self-assessments for goal setting, formulating plans, researching, revising plans, and working together. These self-assessments were in the form of group planning guides and group evaluation sheets (see Figures 4.6 and 4.7).

We assessed individual as well as group work. There was individual self-assessment of participation in project work in the form of journal writing, surveys, and checklists. There was group evaluation of group work. There was teacher assessment of individual performance in group work, which provided for individual accountability within the group. There was individual, ongoing feedback from students regarding content, activities, and rubrics. Feedback was in the form of journal writing, surveys, and group processing. All of this helped evaluate the processes involved in our learning.

## GROUP PLANNING GUIDE
A McHome Team Creation

GROUP # _____                                        Date: _____

NAMES: _____

| Goal(s) for Today: | | | |
|---|---|---|---|
| **Done?** | **WHAT IS TO BE DONE?** | **HOW?** | **BY WHOM?** |
| (Check off as you complete each task.) | (Make a list of all tasks to be done today in order to reach your above goal(s).) | (What do you need to get the job done, for example, materials, resources, etc. to meet your above goal(s)?) | (Who will be completing this task?) |

EVALUATION: (How did your group work today? What did you do right? What did you do wrong?) ___

_____
_____
_____
_____

REVISIONS: (If you did not reach your goal(s) today, how will you change your plan?) ___

_____
_____
_____
_____

**Figure 4.6.** Team-developed group planning guide.

## CONCLUSION

When teachers are advocating new ways in which to learn (e.g., integrating the curriculum) and new ways to demonstrate learning (e.g., alternative assessments), conflicts often occur between the teacher's role as "encourager" of students' efforts to branch out and take risks and the role

## GROUP   EVALUATION   SHEET
### A McHome Team Creation

| | Always | 10 |
|---|---|---|
| | Mostly | 9 |
| | Sometimes | 8 |
| | Never | 0 |

Group #_____

| | TOTAL | I contributed my ideas and information | I asked others for their ideas and information | I summarized all our ideas and information | I shared my materials with teammates | I asked for help when I needed it | I helped the other members of my group learn | I made sure everyone in my group understood how to do the task | I included everyone in our work | I helped keep the group on task | I worked with my group until all came to concensus |
|---|---|---|---|---|---|---|---|---|---|---|---|
| DATE: | | | | | | | | | | | |
| | | | | | | | | | | | |
| | | | | | | | | | | | |
| | | | | | | | | | | | |
| DATE: | | | | | | | | | | | |
| | | | | | | | | | | | |
| | | | | | | | | | | | |
| | | | | | | | | | | | |
| DATE: | | | | | | | | | | | |
| | | | | | | | | | | | |
| | | | | | | | | | | | |
| | | | | | | | | | | | |
| DATE: | | | | | | | | | | | |
| | | | | | | | | | | | |
| | | | | | | | | | | | |
| | | | | | | | | | | | |
| DATE: | | | | | | | | | | | |
| | | | | | | | | | | | |
| | | | | | | | | | | | |
| | | | | | | | | | | | |
| | | | | | | | | | | | |

**Figure 4.7.** Group evaluation sheet.

of "judge" of students' efforts/performances. It is difficult for a teacher to be both an encourager and a judge. Because performance assessments are new to students and teachers alike, grading can be a difficult task. Teachers want to encourage students to take risks but students want to cling to the familiar or traditional assessments. In addition, alternative assessments are usually more difficult for students than traditional assessments because students must demonstrate higher-order thinking skills. These two factors together—the newness of the assessments as well as the higher level of difficulty—may contribute to students' grades taking a temporary "dip." That is why it is important for students to have opportunities to collaborate in the development of the assessments and the rubrics. This way they will know ahead of time what they must do to succeed. They should also have opportunities to "redo" when it is appropriate.

When asked, "How do you feel about using rubrics for assessment as opposed to traditional tests?" one of our students responded, "I like the other ways of grading, not rubrics, because you write less and it's less work." Another student simply stated, "It's harder." But most of our students had comments similar to the following: "I like it a lot better because you're not put under as much pressure and you learn things better than you do with the others." Another student added, "I liked the rubrics better because sometimes you don't know what's on some of your tests, so I think it's to our benefit." The value of an assessment, then, is the degree to which it provides students with a perspective on their learning.

# Chapter 5

# COMPONENT: CONTENT INTEGRATION

During the quest, our curriculum was becoming coherent. Our students indicated they were being challenged, becoming more responsible, becoming more self-directed, seeing their learning connecting to the world outside of the classroom, becoming independent learners, learning to work with others, and actively engaging in their own learning. The following are some of the responses our students made during small-group interviews with Elizabeth (November 1992) when asked the question, "How are you being taught this year in relationship to your previous education?"

- The students [help] choose the curriculum. There's a lot of group work.
- This year is more interesting. We have no books. We can see the applicability. It is hard to get used to. We have an integrated academic block, making connections. Sometimes it is science and sometimes it is social studies.
- We have a choice in what we want to do. We are going out on our own, without a teacher leading us every place. It's easier on students, more interesting. We can effectively communicate with other people and with groups. We are learning to solve problems that come up. We are learning traditional skills as well as new things. It is good preparation for high school.
- We get to be ourselves. We work in groups or as individuals. There is not just one grade. It is more real life. We get to work with other

people. We learn from the other students when they make presentations, etc.

- It is easier. We have more discussion rather than the teacher explaining and then giving you homework.... We are learning more about real life and not so much about the past. We are more active. We are learning adult roles. We are learning to be a self-directed achiever and an involved citizen.
- It is not as structured as old-fashioned teaching. We learn adult skills—how to communicate effectively, contribute, and control yourself. It has affected us a lot. It has made us more mature. It has prepared us for high school. Our parents think this is preparing us for high school. At first I didn't like it. I didn't trust the teacher. The first few days we made guidelines. We thought we would just discuss all the time. Now we are doing projects, communicating, becoming closer. There's a lot less discipline. We get to make up our own rules, our own consequences. Students can't say it's not fair.
- We work a lot in groups. We can redo everything if we turn it in on time. We get to make our own rules. The teachers in the past used to tell us when it's due, what it is to look like, etc. Now they just tell us when it is due. The rest is on our own. At the beginning of the year it was confusing, but it got better. There is a lot of decision making. It will help us choose classes in high school and in careers. Our parents approve. There is a lot of organization. We are assuming adult roles. You get to know everybody better. There is peer-on-peer learning. It is easier. You listen more to your peers than teachers.

These student comments reiterated our overarching goal of integrating the curriculum. In order to integrate curriculum, one of the first things we had to do was arrive at an understanding of what content was. Content, in the context of our integrated curriculum, involved everything the students needed and wanted to know and do in order to make sense of themselves and the world around them. It involved addressing students' personal and social concerns. Peer relationships, racism, and child abuse were examples of our students' concerns. Content involved answering questions about those concerns: How do people learn to get along? What are the factors that contribute to child abuse? Content involved learning how to acquire new knowledge: How do I pursue the answers to my questions? This new knowledge included learning facts, skills, and concepts from the disciplines of knowledge and their representative school subject areas (e.g., social studies, language arts, science, fine arts, and math). Beane (1995b) maintained, "A discipline of knowledge is a field of inquiry about some aspect of the world—the physical world, the flow of events over time, numeric structures, and so on" (p. 617). Content also involved demonstration of knowledge. Demonstration of knowledge was embedded in the curriculum and was not separate.

In addition to our thinking of what content was in curriculum integration, other factors influenced our curriculum, including county curriculum reform, administrative support, resources, state-mandated curriculum, and time. For example, our county was involved in social studies curriculum reform. Elaine was a member of the county's Social Studies Restructuring Committee whose task was to rewrite the K–12 social studies curriculum. As a result of the county curriculum reform efforts, the eighth-grade curriculum was structured around themes. During our quest for coherent curriculum, we chose some of these themes for investigation.

Local school administrative support also affected our efforts. Our assistant principal was supportive from the very beginning of our quest for coherent curriculum. For example, we were given the opportunity to form a two-teacher team and the flexibility to develop our own schedules.

Availability of resources was also a factor that influenced our curriculum. Our students soon discovered they would have to go way beyond the classroom materials to answer their questions. A group of four students wrote a proposal requesting (and receiving) funds for an online computer service.

As all educators know, state-mandated curriculum impacts classroom curriculum. However, as we learned in working through this process, state-mandated curriculum objectives do *not* have to dictate the classroom curriculum—they did not dictate ours. Instead we *used* the state-mandated curriculum objectives, knowing when, where, and how these objectives fit to support coherence.

Time is always a factor in curriculum development. Our quest for coherent curriculum took an enormous amount of time on the part of students and teachers. However, we were all so absorbed by the work we were doing that we really didn't focus on the amount of time that was involved. Instead, we focused on the curriculum. Our curriculum themes were centered around student social concerns, current high-interest topics, environmental concerns, and economic concerns.

## MODELING INTEGRATION OF CONTENT

It was important that our students know more about the curriculum development process so they could become personally involved. In this section of the chapter we share how we modeled this process that included addressing student concerns, answering questions, and learning how to acquire new knowledge.

## Content: Addressing Student Concerns

We began planning our initial unit by modeling the first step in the curriculum design process (Step 1: deciding on the theme of study). We utilized the Rising Eighth-Grade Surveys to help identify possible themes for our first unit. Many of the students had expressed an interest in finding out more about themselves. To help our students find out more about themselves, their families, and their heritage, we chose the theme Human Migration. The focus of the Human Migration unit was on why people migrated in the past and present (e.g., employment, religious freedom, wealth, political freedom) and the effects of human migration on their future.

## Content: Answering Questions

We modeled for our students the next step in the curriculum design process (Step 2: developing focus questions). We wanted our students to realize that these questions guide the learning process. For the Human Migration unit the questions we explored included: How are individuals impacted by human migration? How have human migration patterns correlated with the colonization of the United States and Georgia? What are some present and future trends for human migration and its implications upon an increasingly interdependent world?

## Content: Learning How to Acquire New Knowledge

We then brainstormed with the students about the skills they might need to work on while they were exploring their questions regarding human migration (Step 3: linking skills to content). For example, students identified group processing skills (e.g., active listening, restating, questioning). In previous years, our students had worked in groups. But that did not necessarily mean they had been taught skills needed for successful group work. Using the T-chart strategy, we brainstormed "active listening" descriptors (see Figure 5.1).

Our students also identified research skills (e.g., interviewing, data collecting, synthesizing) and communication skills (e.g., writing for clarity, writing for a purpose, writing for an audience) as being important. Students practiced group processing skills, research skills, and communication skills as they investigated how and why their families came to America.

## Content: Demonstration of Knowledge

We wanted the students to realize that there were all kinds of ways to demonstrate their knowledge. Because we had a democratic classroom, we wanted them to have choices regarding how they wanted to demonstrate

## Active Listening

| looks like | sounds like |
|---|---|
| smiling at speaker | saying, "unhuh" |
| nodding your head | asking questions |
| positive body language | asking for clarification |
| eye contact | |
| sitting up straight | |

**Figure 5.1.** Active listening descriptors.

their knowledge (Step 4: performance assessment). For example, they could choose to create a 10-frame Nickelodeon (pictures and scripts) or they could choose to write a true or fictionalized short story describing what they imagined their ancestors' immigration trip to America was like. We modeled for the students how to create evaluation checklists. They used these checklists to evaluate their Nickelodeons or their short stories.

All students wrote a paper on the implications of future migration on themselves and on the United States. We (students and teachers) cocreated a performance evaluation rubric for the paper. The rubric included criteria for content, mechanics, and connection to the theme of study. Again, we were modeling the construction and use of appropriate evaluation measures (see Figure 5.2).

In order for the students to be able to gain the skills and knowledge needed for the performance assessment, which addressed the focus questions, we created learning activities (Step 5: learning activities). Some of these activities included creating a migration map showing the influences of ocean and wind currents on early ocean voyages, a data retrieval chart showing the varying reasons for colony settlement, and a treasure chest of word origins.

The last step in the curriculum design process was locating appropriate resources (Step 6: resources). We gave our students blank pathfinders. A pathfinder is a strategy useful for keeping track of reference materials. Traditionally, for units of study, teachers collect appropriate resources for their students to use. We wanted our students to know how to use the technol-

# RESEARCH PAPER RUBRIC
### A McHome Team Creation

Name:_____              Date:_____

| Research Based Content | | | | Item Weight | Item Total |
|---|---|---|---|---|---|
| 1<br>Answers 1-2<br>Questions | 2<br>Answers 3-5<br>Questions | 3<br>Answers 6-7<br>Questions | 4<br>Answers All 8<br>Questions | X_____ = | _____ |

Bibliography

| 1<br>1-2 Sources | 2<br>3 Sources/<br>Incorrect Format | 3<br>3 Sources/<br>Correct Format | 4<br>4+Sources/<br>Correct Format | X_____ = | _____ |
|---|---|---|---|---|---|

Originality

| | | | 4<br>Clearly States in<br>Own Words/Cites<br>all Quotes | X_____ = | _____ |
|---|---|---|---|---|---|

Spelling

| 1<br>11 or More<br>Words<br>Misspelled | 2<br>6-10 Words<br>Misspelled | 3<br>1-5 Words<br>Misspelled | 4<br>Overall<br>Correct<br>Spelling | X_____ = | _____ |
|---|---|---|---|---|---|

Neatness

| 1<br>Illegible | 2<br>Messy; Poor<br>Spacing;<br>Wrong Format;<br>Hard to Read | 3<br>Clear and<br>Legible | 4<br>Very Neat<br>and Easy to<br>Read | X_____ = | _____ |
|---|---|---|---|---|---|

**TOTAL** _____

**Figure 5.2.** Performance evaluation rubric for the paper.

ogy available in the media center (e.g., microfiche, online card catalog, CD-ROM) to locate all available appropriate resources for themselves. We wanted our students to gain skills that would help them to be active participants in their own learning. For an example of a pathfinder, see Figure 5.3.

At an end-of-the-unit team meeting, we discussed the curriculum design process with our students. We wanted to know if they understood this process and how they felt about it.

```
                        ╭─────────────────────────────╮
                        │   A McHome Team PathFinder    │
                        ╰─────────────────────────────╯
```

| Topic | Human Migration will be examined through the study of people moving from one place to another for political, economic, environmental, and social reasons. Catalysts for human migration will be viewed from the essential family unit in Georgia to world movement patterns. We will examine the political, economic, social/religious and environmental reasons for Human Migration past, present and future. |
|---|---|
| **Subject Headings** | |
| **Newspaper Articles** | |
| **Encyclopedias** | |
| **Books** | |
| **Periodical Indexes** | |
| **Vertical File** | |

**Figure 5.3.** PathFinder.

In a critique of the curriculum design format, some students wrote:

- The designing down is a good idea because it gives us an organization in our work. It also helps us on deciding what and how we will do our presentation.
- The designing down sheet is the page where you mainly design your whole project, and plan out what you are going to do. It helped us

because sometimes we would forget about having to do something, then we could just look back on it, and it would remind us.
- The designing down format is a process to simplify a presentation. It got us organized so we knew what to do and not get off track.
- I used it to help me better understand what was going to be on my project and how I was going to do it.
- My group used it to show what we were going to teach in our mini-lesson. Our mini-lesson was very clear after we finished our designing down form. We wrote down everything we were going to do and did it. It was so helpful it got us a 94, plus 5 extra points, so a final grade of 99! On the designing down form are a list of boxes in a certain order. I think they are in a logical order so that I don't get confused with what I'm doing. This is brand new to me [planning curriculum] so it was like a gift when they put the boxes in this order. This was a good idea, because it gave me a crystal-clear idea of what I'm doing.

It was clear to us from their comments about "designing down" that our students understood curriculum planning. We were ready for our first student–teacher cocreated curriculum unit.

## INTEGRATING CONTENT WITHIN THEMATIC UNITS

In this section of the chapter, we will discuss the remaining thematic units in relationship to the content as we have defined it. For each unit we provide a rationale for the unit and examples of how the content was integrated. We have intentionally separated the aspects of content for clarification purposes.

### Human Interactions

The Human Interactions unit was a study of social issues and concerns that affected us personally, as well as issues that affected societies in the past. As part of the Human Interactions unit the students selected for study issues of personal concern. Examples of issues they investigated include racism, abortion rights, and world hunger.

A group of five girls chose animal testing as their topic. Each of the examples to follow are taken from the group's curriculum design plan.

*Content: Addressing student concerns*
- Animal Testing

*Content: Answering questions*
- How are Human Interactions (Animal Testing) affecting my world?

   1. What is animal testing?
   2. Why do laboratories use animal testing?
   3. What are some of the animals used in animal testing?
   4. What type of research is conducted and what kinds of tests are run on animals?
   5. Why do laboratories believe it is necessary to use animals in research and testing?
   6. Why are some people against using animals in laboratory research?
   7. What are some of the damaging effects toward the animals?
   8. What is animal research?
   9. How much money is spent yearly (approximately) on animal testing and research?
   10. How does animal testing and research affect the world around us?
   11. What types of products are tested on animals?

*Content: Learning how to acquire new knowledge*
- Data Collection/Technology
- Group Processing
- Writing a Rubric
- Writing a Connection Statement
- Listening Skills
- Speaking Effectively
- Organization
- Writing a Plan
- Polite Phone Calls

*Content: Demonstration of knowledge*
- Development of Curriculum Design Plan
- Journals
- Letter Writing
- Opinion Sheets
- Posters
- Group Presentation
- Student-Designed Rubric
- Project Portfolio

## Human Interactions and the Environment

Our students were so interested in their study of current social issues affect-ing them that they wanted to continue their studies to include environmental issues of social concern. Topics students chose to learn about included erosion due to clear cutting (selective harvesting), acid rain, and quality of air and water.

A group of three boys chose smog, ozone depletion, radiation, and the relation among the three as their topic. The following examples are taken from the group's curriculum design plan.

*Content: Addressing student concerns*
- Smog, ozone depletion, radiation, and the relation among the three

*Content: Answering questions*
- How does smog, ozone depletion, and radiation affect the earth?

SMOG
1. Where does it come from?
2. What does it do?
3. Where does it happen?
4. When did people start working against it?
5. How can it be stopped, slowed, or reduced?
6. How does it affect Georgia?

SOLAR RADIATION
1. How is it distributed?
2. Where does it come from?
3. Where does it go?
4. What are the effects on plants and animals in Georgia?
5. How can it be stopped?

OZONE DEPLETION
1. How does it occur?
2. How does it affect the people of Georgia?
3. How can we stop it?
4. Where does it come from?
5. When did people discover it happening?
6. How does it affect life in general?

*Content: Learning how to acquire new knowledge*
- Write Good Research Questions
- Write for Information
- Interview

- Find Sources
- Incorporate Technology
- Teach Mini-Lesson to Class
- Notetaking
- Synthesizing Information

*Content: Demonstration of knowledge*
- Development of Curriculum Design Plan
- Mini-Lesson
- Posters
- Group Presentation
- Student-Designed Rubric
- Project Portfolio
- Puppet Show
- HyperCard Stack

## Human and Civil Rights and Responsibilities

In the Human and Civil Rights and Responsibilities unit, we examined the relationships among past, present, and future human and civil rights issues from the 1600s to the present. Examples of issues and events studied included the Salem Witch Trials, Industrial Revolution, pre–Civil War conditions, and the Balkan crisis. Issues and events in this unit were studied by all students on the McHome Team.

*Content: Addressing student concerns*
- Human and Civil Rights and Responsibilities

*Content: Answering questions*
- What are historical and current examples of events that fulfill/ deny basic human and civil rights and what were their effects upon society?

*Content: Learning how to acquire new knowledge*
- Utilizing Learning Strategies
- Analyzing Information
- Critical Thinking
- Oral and Written Communication
- Note taking
- Reading
- Group Processing

*Content: Demonstration of knowledge*
- Worksheets
- Group Presentations
- Discussions
- Peace Conference
- Simulation
- Living History Timeline

## Leadership

Our Leadership unit was originally designed to examine the qualities of leadership and the impact of 20th-century leaders (individuals and groups) upon our society/world. However, because of the time of the school year (February and March) and because we (students and teachers) were mentally exhausted from the previous four units, we chose to depart from our original unit. Instead we chose to do a novel study of the book *Jurassic Park* (Crichton, 1990), incorporating, the qualities of leadership when possible.

*Content: Addressing student concerns*
- Enjoy Reading a Novel

*Content: Answering questions*
- What are the leadership qualities of the different characters of the book and how did the characters affect each other?
- How would the entire world be affected if the proposed "prehistoric theme park" opened as scheduled?

*Content: Learning how to acquire new knowledge*
- Reading
- Discussions
- Gathering Information
- Generating Hypotheses

*Content: Demonstration of knowledge*
- Student Hands-on Science Labs
- Essays
- Diagrams
- Advertisement Brochures
- Bulletin Board Murals
- Timelines

- Tests
- Topographic Maps
- Plot Line

## Communities of the Future

Our final unit of the year was Communities of the Future. It was our intention that, for this final unit, the students would take on most of the decision-making responsibilities. We wanted the students to practice working on skills that would help them become more self-directed.

*Content: Addressing student concerns*
- The Future

*Content: Answering questions*
- What is needed for society to function?
- If you are going to begin a new colony/community in the future, what would be involved?

  1. What kind of government and economic system is in your community of the future?
  2. What is your vision for education in your community of the future?
  3. What type of shelter would you have in your community of the future?
  4. What energy sources would you utilize in your community of the future?
  5. What food sources would be available in your community of the future?
  6. What division of labor would you utilize in your community of the future?

*Content: Learning how to acquire new knowledge*
- Developing Good Research Questions
- Using a Variety of Resources
- Interpreting Information from a Variety of Media
- Writing to Communicate Information
- Group Processing
- Cooperation
- Teamwork
- Listening
- Contributing Ideas
- Encouraging Others
- Organizing Work

- Keeping Neat Records
- Developing Individual and Group Plans
- Revising Plans
- Using Time Wisely
- Reflecting

*Content: Demonstration of knowledge*
- Personal Journals
- HyperCard Stacks
- Slide Shows
- Scale Model
- 3-D Model
- Rubrics
- Group Portfolios

## CONCLUSION

Our students were being challenged, becoming more responsible for themselves and their learning, becoming more self-directed, seeing their learning connected to the world outside the classroom, becoming independent learners, learning to work with others, actively engaging in their own learning, and having fun. Integrating the content largely contributed to making the curriculum coherent.

Again, content, in the context of our integrated curriculum, involved everything the students needed and wanted to know and do in order to make sense of themselves and the world around them. It involved addressing students' personal and social concerns. Content involved answering questions about those concerns. Content involved learning how to acquire new knowledge. Content also involved demonstration of knowledge.

In each of our units we integrated the content. Integrating the content helped facilitate the realization of our goals:

- Develop a curriculum that gives students and teachers a deeper understanding of content.
- Make connections between school and the outside world.
- Guide students in the learning process.
- Encourage students to accept responsibilities.
- Help students to learn to work effectively with a diversity of people.
- Encourage students to take risks and learn from mistakes.
- Assist students in becoming effective problem solvers.
- Enable students to discover that learning can be fun.

# Chapter 6

# COMPONENT: PEDAGOGY

Pedagogical knowledge refers to knowledge the individual possesses about the domain of teaching. On the McHome Team, pedagogy involved matching the curriculum to the needs of the students. We did this by utilizing a variety of teaching and learning strategies—strategies that made their educational experiences coherent.

In this chapter we share some of the strategies that were utilized during the Human and Civil Rights and Responsibilities unit. Sample strategies used included brainstorming, storytelling, Jigsaw, data retrieval chart, simulation, collaborative problem solving, and making connections.

The Human and Civil Rights and Responsibilities unit evolved from the McHome students' concerns about race relationships they had investigated in the unit on Human Interactions. They wanted to know more about racism in America. They wanted to know why our society is the way it is. They asked, "Why can't people get along in America?" They were also concerned and interested about their own personal rights. They questioned their rights as teenagers. For example, there is a curfew in our town, young people are not allowed to congregate in the mall, and it seemed to them that their actions were always being questioned. In other words, they felt adults were always suspicious of their looks, their actions, and their motivations. They wanted to know what rights they, as teenagers, had.

## STRATEGY: BRAINSTORMING

The first strategy utilized in this unit was brainstorming. The students got into small groups and brainstormed a list of what they felt should be their rights. After about 20 minutes, we got back together as a whole group and compiled all the lists. Examples included: "I have the right to say whatever I want," "I have the right to write whatever I want," "I have the right to an education," and "I have the right to do whatever I want." Then we began discussing these rights.

> ELAINE: So, you're telling me I have the right to do whatever I want to do? Okay. If I want to drive 80 miles per hour through a school zone, I can. It's my right.
> Students: [shocked!] You can't do that. You'd hurt somebody.
> Elaine: Then you're telling me that with rights come responsibilities?
> Students: Well, yeah. Okay.
> Elaine: Then maybe we need to say what those responsibilities are.

The students got back into brainstorming groups and "fleshed out" responsibilities that went along with rights. We discussed these rights and responsibilities and, as a team, created the McHome Team Rights and Responsibilities list (see Figure 6.1).

This process was an example of democracy in our classroom: We guided and challenged our students' thinking; we did not presume to tell them what to think.

## STRATEGY: MAKING CONNECTIONS

For this unit, it would have been simple for us to ask the students to take their textbook and read about significant events in history that influenced human and civil rights. But, because this was integrated, coherent curriculum, the development of the unit came from the need to know by the students. The students kept asking questions about race relations and racism in America. They saw a need to go back in time and find the causes. It was important to investigate the Industrial Revolution because the Industrial Revolution provided answers as to why slavery became prominent in America. Because Colonial Georgians had used slaves, we saw the need to examine how and why slavery occurred here as well.

Our state was greatly influenced during the Industrial Revolution because of the increased demand for cotton in the textile mills of Great Britain. Colonial Georgian cotton farmers utilized slaves to fill the demand for cheap labor.

Through our continuing study, the students were beginning to understand connections between the Industrial Revolution, slavery, race relations, and how society was affected. They saw a need to know more about the past.

| I Have the Right to: | I Have the Responsibility to: |
|---|---|
| Free speech | Tell the truth |
| | Not put others down |
| | Not verbally abuse others |
| | Not damage others' reputations |
| | Not to exploit others (such as handicapped) |
| | Not infringe upon the rights of others |
| | Be considerate |
| | Respect the right of others to have free speech |
| Equal treatment | Treat others equally |
| | Not discriminate against others because of gender, religion, race, origin, or size |
| Freedom of thought (be able to write whatever I want) | Respect the thoughts of others |
| | Write the truth |
| | Not make fun of others |
| | Be considerate |
| | Think of the feelings of others |
| Be respected | Respect others |
| | Be kind to others |
| | Act in such a way that lets people respect me |
| | Talk to others in a respectful tone |
| Learn | Come to class |
| | Not bother anyone else |
| | Contribute to a pleasant learning environment |
| | Study |
| | Be willing to learn |
| | Listen |
| | Let the teacher teach |
| | Help the teacher teach me |
| | Do my work |
| Do whatever I want | Not hurt others by what I do |
| | Do the right thing |
| | Respect the right of others to be whatever they want to be |
| | Work hard |
| Be whatever I want | Respect the right of others to be whatever they want to be |
| | Work hard |
| Be Happy | Not ruin other people's happiness |
| | Not gain my happiness at the expense of other people's sadness |
| Privacy | Respect the privacy of others |

**Figure 6.1.** The McHome Team Rights and Responsibilities.

## STRATEGY: STORYTELLING

We wanted our students to get a realistic view of slavery and to personally identify with the plight of the slave. Because storytelling is motivational, attention-getting, and brings issues and ideas to life, we decided to utilize this strategy to help each student personally identify with the plight of the slave. We watched and discussed Alex Haley's miniseries *Roots*. To provide a background for the miniseries, we discussed Alex Haley and his compelling desire to find out about his own family history—his "roots." This story was a semibiographical account of his own family history.

We purposely did not give our students terms to define or questions to answer as they viewed the first part of *Roots* because we wanted their full concentration so that they could personally connect with the character Kunta Kinte. They saw Kunta Kinte as a friend, a son, a grandson, a brother, a young maturing teenager, just like young people today. They all liked Kunta Kinte.

We stopped the video at the part where Kunta Kinte was captured. He was on the beach in chains; he looked and saw the slave ship and the ocean behind it. At that moment, he realized his fate: he would never see his family, friends, or home again.

Then, without any discussion, we asked the students to respond in writing to the following statements: "You are Kunta Kinte. Tell me what you're thinking. Tell me what you're feeling." Their written responses were compelling. The students had personally connected with this desperately lonely, frightened, and shattered human being.

No other strategy could have been as powerful in making this connection as storytelling. This story really made "history come alive" for our students. Because of this experience, our students came away with a more realistic view of slavery through their personal identification with the plight of a slave. They felt a need to know even more about the past.

## STRATEGY: MAKING CONNECTIONS

As a team, we were beginning to gain a greater understanding of our present society as a result of studying the past. Because *Roots* encompassed the American Revolution, further questions were raised. For example, What led the colonists to rebel? What were the causes of the American Revolution? What were the effects on society?

To help our students get a better mental picture of the events that led to the American Revolution they created cause and effect brochures depicting the "Road to the American Revolution." In this learning activity (and also assessment), they depicted events from the end of the French and Indian War to the Battle of Lexington.

Connections were made between each event depicted. Through these activities, the students were again seeing connections: the Industrial Revolution, slavery, race relations, political representation, civil disobedience, and their effects upon society.

## STRATEGY: JIGSAW

In our discussion of our own state's history, the treatment of the Cherokee stands out as a prime example of how a society can be adversely affected by lack of human and civil rights protection. Our students were vaguely aware of the mistreatment of the Georgia Cherokee at the hands of the government. What they couldn't understand was why. They wanted to know how we could be so cruel to innocent people. To help them understand how this happened, we utilized a Jigsaw strategy. Our students formed small groups. Each group was responsible for learning about a segment of Cherokee history. Each group then shared what they learned with the whole team. As they shared their insights, they gained a better understanding of how and why the eventual, forced removal of the Cherokee from Georgia, the Trail of Tears, happened.

## STRATEGY: DATA RETRIEVAL CHART

After our students had an understanding of how the Cherokee came to be forcefully removed from Georgia, we turned our attention to yet another event from our past that would help us understand our present society: the Civil War.

Our students thought that the war had one cause: slavery. They needed to know the whole story. To help them gain a better understanding, we gave them a Data Retrieval Chart to complete. The chart provided the students with four conflicting issues that eventually led to war: Slavery and the Abolitionists, Tariffs, Settling of the West, and States' Rights.

The team broke up into groups of four. Each group worked together to complete the chart. It was important to their understanding of the eventual conflict that they examine each issue from both perspectives: North and South. After the groups had completed their assignment, we got together as a team, discussed their findings, and compiled a team chart (see Figure 6.2).

This learning experience was meaningful to the students because they had to work together to find the information. It wasn't given to them in a lecture or by reading a packet of teacher-prepared material.

| ISSUE | NORTH | SOUTH |
|---|---|---|
| Slavery and the Abolitionists | Most Northerners did not care about the slave issue. A small group, abolitionists, wanted to see slavery ended. Many Northerners did not want slavery extended into the new territories and states. | Most Southerners did not own any slaves. They supported slavery because they saw it as a symbol of wealth and power. Therefore slavery was supported by most Southerners. |
| Tariffs | The North favored protective tariffs to protect their industries against foreign competition. | Southerners had few industries to protect. They relied heavily upon imported manufactured goods. They resented the North being able to place high tariffs on the goods they needed to import. |
| Settling of the West | The North preferred the government sell land cheap. They also favored developing the West (roads and canals) at the expense of the government (taxes). Some Northern factory owners feared losing workers. | The South wanted the new lands for farming because the land was rich, the climate good, and rivers were just right for transporting products. Southerners wanted the land distributed cheaply and quickly. The South did not want taxes to go up to develop the West. |
| States' Rights | Northerners argued that the states had no power to declare a U.S. law null and void. States had no right to secede. | The South said that each state had the right to determine if a law passed by Congress should be obeyed. If a state decided a law was unconstitutional they could declare the law null and void (nullification). They said that each state had the right to secede (withdraw) from the Union. |

**Figure 6.2.** Data retrieval chart.

## STRATEGY: SIMULATION

One of the most volatile issues surrounding the Civil War was the right to own slaves. The Dred Scott case (the issue of ownership surrounding slavery) escalated tensions between the North and South. We decided to incorporate a simulation of the Dred Scott court case, to help make these historical events "come alive" for our students.

At this point, the students did not know the outcome of the Dred Scott decision. For our simulation, two students played the role of the defense, two students played the role of the plaintiff's attorneys, Elaine played the role of the judge, and the rest of the team played the role of the jury.

The defense and plaintiff teams were provided with all facts surrounding the case. Instead of planning strategy separately, the four students got together and scripted their roles. Elaine was originally supposed to keep the trial moving according to judicial procedures. Instead, the "attorneys" took complete control (it was much better than originally intended). The simulation was exciting and fast-paced.

After hearing both sides present their case, the "jury" deliberated and came to a verdict: Dred Scott was a free man. The "jury" explained their reasoning behind the verdict: no one has a right to own someone else, period. We had to explain to our students that this was not the verdict handed down by the United States Supreme Court. The Supreme Court justices found in favor of the plaintiff; Dred Scott remained a slave. This led to a heated debate about human and civil rights in America, then and now.

## STRATEGY: MAKING CONNECTIONS

As we looked at early 20th-century America, we learned even more about the ongoing struggle for human and civil rights (e.g., disenfranchisement of black voters, women's suffrage, child labor, segregation of schools). These issues led us to investigate the Civil Rights Movement in America. Our students learned about *Brown vs. The Board of Education,* the Montgomery bus boycott, sit-down demonstrations at Southern lunch counters, and much more. These events highlighted the continuing struggle to secure rights for all Americans.

Gaining a historical perspective gave our students a deeper insight into contemporary American society. Our students began to understand why we study history: the past helps us understand the present.

## STRATEGY: COLLABORATIVE PROBLEM SOLVING

Implementing coherent curriculum involves bringing into the classroom current issues and events. Our students wanted to know about the war in Bosnia. They wanted to know why people who had just gained their freedom from a repressive dictatorship would wage war on each other. Again, a historical perspective was necessary to understand the current situation. So, in order to gain a historical perspective on the war in Bosnia, we used the strategy of collaborative problem solving. We had our students participate in a "Bosnian Peace Conference."

We provided background information for our students. We brought in current newspaper and magazine articles that explained the history of the current situation. Our students analyzed, discussed, and synthesized the information in the articles. After they had an understanding of the entire situation, they got into "delegation groups" to draw up a peace plan. Using what they knew about the Bosnian people and their past, each group generated a new map of the region and plan for peace. Each group of delegates shared their ideas with the whole team and substantiated their reasoning.

The war in Bosnia was yet another example of the continuing struggle for human and civil rights.

## CONCLUSION

The culminating event of this unit was the Living History Timeline, a series of vignettes (chosen by the students) depicting human and civil rights struggles throughout history. In addition to performing for each other, our students also performed the Living History Timeline for nine other classes in the school. Having an audience beyond our own classroom added yet another dimension to their learning.

The strategies used in this unit helped make learning interesting, fun, motivating, and personally relevant for our students. There was a considerable difference between studying history the traditional way (reading about issues and events in a textbook) and the way our students learned about the past. Our students looked at the issues and events of the past as being indispensable to understanding today's society.

# Chapter 7

# COMPONENT: COMMUNICATION

As we went through the process of developing a coherent curriculum, it was important to establish and maintain effective communication. To us, effective communication meant exchanging ideas, feelings, interests, and knowledge. In this chapter, we share examples of a variety of ways communication was achieved.

## COMMUNICATION WITH STUDENTS

On the McHome Team communication with our students was ongoing. We encouraged them to express their concerns, feelings, and ideas. We discussed issues together as a team, in small groups, and one-on-one. "Student voice" was very important. We worked on student input throughout the school year.

When needed, we held small group or individual conferences with students implementing a modified version of our school's conference form (see Figure 7.1). This conference form was adapted to student and classroom needs and concerns. Through this process, students and teachers learned more about being effective communicators. This conferencing process established clear teacher/student expectations and intentions.

To maintain communications during project work time, we established group conferencing. For example, during the Human Interactions and the Environment unit, students were divided into groups based on their chosen

Conference _____     Date: _____
Attendees:    _____     Time: _____

Purpose of Conference: _____
_____
_____

Background Information: _____
_____
_____

NEEDS ASSESSMENT:

| Things we are doing now : | Things we need to do: |
|---|---|
| | |
| | |
| | |
| | |

Plan of Action:
_____
_____
_____
_____
_____

Signatures:
_____
_____
_____

**Figure 7.1.** Student/Teacher Conference Record form.

environmental concern. During group work time, we mingled around and asked group members various questions such as, "What is your group's goal today?" "What can we do to help?" If the groups were having problems, we would ask more direct, probing questions such as, "Have you found … ?" "Have you called … ?" "Have you looked … ?" or "What sources have you used?" This questioning strategy provided for more effective group processing, group problem solving, and overall project success. Working with students to help them find solutions added depth to their project ideas as well as modeled for students how to evaluate their work; thus, they became more effective problem solvers.

As the school year progressed, we discovered that what students were feeling and what they were willing to communicate verbally were sometimes two different things. To alleviate this problem, we often asked them to reflect in writing. We asked for general or sometimes specific written responses through surveys, questionnaires, or journals. Some examples included student impressions of the first 6 weeks on the McHome Team, student feelings regarding our democratic classroom, thoughts on rubric usage, comparison of performance on traditional versus alternative assessments, and perceptions of integrated curriculum.

Sometimes students were hesitant to voice their concerns or apprehensions during large-group discussions. In order to get input from all students, we often broke up into smaller groupings to brainstorm ideas and solutions. These ideas and solutions were then brought before the whole team as topics for discussion. In this nonthreatening format our students seemed more comfortable communicating their opinions.

Other communications between students and teachers included comments on student work. Students (through peer editing) and teachers shared suggestions for revision/expansion of ideas, the need to reword, and tips for clarifying. These comments provided clear and immediate feedback on student work.

Another form of student/teacher communication was student assignment calendars. Sometimes, as our students wrote in their calendars, we found that they had misinterpreted the assignment. It was helpful to identify and correct misunderstandings at the beginning of the task rather than later on.

Of course, we communicated informally between classes, before school and after school, at lunch, and at break time. This informal type of communication helped us get to know each other on a more personal level.

## COMMUNICATION WITH PARENTS

It was important that parents were kept informed of the McHome Team events in part because curriculum integration was unfamiliar. We (students and teachers) collaborated to communicate better with parents. We informed parents of McHome Team goals, curriculum, and philosophy. Students wrote their parents at the beginning of the school year explaining classroom expectations, the grading policy, and the McHome Team plan for success. Parents initialed a response page (indicating their understanding of team expectations), which was kept on file.

Continuing parent communications involved being updated on student project work, including the use of rubrics. We wanted to let parents know that rubrics were used to guide project work as well as to evaluate performance (see Chapter 4). Parent support was ensured when students took their rubrics home and reviewed them with their parents before beginning their project work. This encouraged comments and questions before project work began, rather than after the project was evaluated. This type of communication was effective because it helped parents better understand our curriculum integration process.

Sometimes there were issues that needed instant communication with parents. For example, if a student was at Step 5 in the management plan (see Chapter 3) we would often have the student phone home. In addition to phone conferencing, we held in-school student/parent/teacher conferences. Students had expressed to us, in previous years, concerns that teachers and parents "talked behind their backs." Therefore, we decided to have both students and parents present at conferences. Often the conference topic was dealt with more effectively when the student was present to answer questions such as, "Why didn't you turn in that assignment?" Having the student present reduced miscommunication between home and school. Communicating effectively between students, parents, and teachers provided a support structure to facilitate coherence.

We also kept a communication log (see Figure 7.2). The log was a great record keeper in that it provided a quick and easy reference for reviewing long-term communication efforts. We sent team newsletters home with every report card. For the newsletters, students contributed articles about their project work. The traditional progress report and report card were also a way of keeping parents in touch.

Additional communications with our parents included PTA meetings (open house, curriculum night, and special programs) throughout the school year. We also had a team information "hot line." This was a phone line for parents or students to call for information related to team activity. Every afternoon, we updated the message to include homework, project due dates, and, occasionally, topics discussed that day in class. It was the students' responsibility to check the "hot line" when they were absent. Parents regularly used this form of communication to keep in touch.

## STUDENT COMMUNICATION WITH OTHERS

Our students often utilized *The Kid's Guide to Social Action* (Lewis, 1991) in their efforts to become more effective communicators. In order for our students to make better use of this resource, we took the book apart and

Student Name:      _____
Parent (s) Name (s): _____
Address: _____
Home Phone Number:    _____
Work Phone Number(s):    _____

                                        _____

| | Date | Person Contacted | Purpose/result of communication |
|---|---|---|---|
| 1. | | | |
| 2. | | | |
| 3. | | | |
| 4. | | | |
| 5. | | | |
| 6. | | | |

**Figure 7.2.** Parent Communication Log Sheet form.

then laminated it onto manila folders. This created a kit for students to use whenever needed. Students found it very useful in preparing interviews, phone calls, surveys, proposals, and business letters.

Due to their involvement in developing their own curriculum, students often had to communicate with experts. They arranged for interviews, phone conferences, field study trips, and guest speakers. For example, during the Human Interactions and the Environment unit, an Environmental Protection Agency (EPA) official was a guest speaker. Since there were a variety of issues under investigation, the students felt it was necessary to have a questioning strategy. They generated a list of questions to be asked, organized them into topics, and selected a student panel to handle the questioning. They developed questions such as, "How does your government office control and regulate ozone pollution?" and "How does your office monitor landfills?" Guests were often surprised at our students' depth of knowledge and questioning skills.

Because of the novelty of curriculum integration, our students were often asked to explain aspects of their project work. For example, in one of our student's foreign-language exploratory classes the teacher was trying to develop a rubric with the students. The teacher was having some difficulty explaining the process, so our student volunteered to help. The following illustrates the knowledge base and communication skills of our student. The teacher stated:

> Recently, after hearing all I thought I needed to know about authentic assessment, and reading everything there is to read about rubrics, my teammate and I decided to let the students in our foreign-language exploratory develop their own rubric to score their projects. I had made an overhead transparency of a simple rubric and explained the value of assessing yourself and your own efforts and what I got from the class were blank faces. My teammate and I were getting nervous; this was not going well.
>
> I knew that one of our eighth-grade teams (Homestead and McGinnis) had done extensive work with their classes with authentic assessment and the development of rubrics and was hoping one of the students from their class would throw in a comment or two.
>
> What I didn't expect was to be rescued by a young girl who raised her hand saying maybe she could help me out. She said that rubrics let you decide what is "excellent" work and that it is an easy way to get a 100. Now, I was skeptical. However, she and her group proceeded to develop a rubric for their group that was far more complicated than my simple example. Her group's rubric assessed much higher-level thinking skills and a professional performance was required for a high score. Naturally, after displaying this group's rubric, the rest of the class was able to follow the lead.
>
> I had been ready to run to Homestead and McGinnis for help, but they had done such an excellent job of teaching that their students were able to teach me.
>
> Jill Williams
> personal communication
> January 29, 1993

## TEACHER COMMUNICATION WITH OTHERS

In order to ensure the success of integrated, coherent curriculum, we knew that clear and positive communication must be established and maintained among the three of us. Gehrke (1991) advised that effective communication between teachers

> require[s] periods of information exchange about basic personal attributes; about individually and commonly held interests and talents; about their current subject-area teaching goals, themes, and organizing concept; and about their general academic knowledge-level expertise. (p. 116)

It was also important that the McHome Team involve our assistant principal in our quest for coherent curriculum. Her support of our program was reflected in meetings with McHome Team students and parents. The nature of communication between us and our administrator was open and honest. We met weekly with her to discuss student concerns, parent concerns, and classroom procedures. She made many classroom visits, some at our request, some at our students' requests, and some her own idea.

## CONCLUSION

For curriculum to become coherent, it was necessary for students, parents, teachers, and others involved to communicate effectively. As a result of our year-long efforts, we learned to share our educational philosophy, goals, expectations, frustrations, and successes.

**Chapter 8**

# COMPONENT: SCHEDULING AND ORGANIZATIONAL STRUCTURES

Embedded within this chapter are the facets of effective scheduling and organizational structures that were essential for promoting coherence on the McHome Team. How we developed our two-teacher team, team teaching, class schedules, and classroom settings are shared.

## TWO-TEACHER TEAM

We discovered many advantages to having a two-teacher team and only 58 students. We were able to know each student individually, incorporate alternative assessments, develop personalized studies, utilize flexible scheduling, and conduct team meetings. Alexander (1995, p. 7) stated that two-teacher team structures directly address several middle school issues:

1. Two-person teaching teams support block scheduling. Teachers don't have to vie for equal time slots to deliver their content and students don't have to change classes every 45 to 50 minutes.
2. Two-person teaching teams provide flexibility. Students and teachers can be grouped in a variety of ways. We have found that 40–60 students is a manageable number for large group activities. In addition, one teacher can supervise a large group while the other teacher can meet with individual students or smaller groups.

3. Close relationships between students and teachers develop naturally throughout the school day, and advisor–advisee functions can be integrated into the larger curriculum.
4. Coordinating team activities becomes easier with a smaller number of teachers. Team teaching requires an enormous amount of coordination, communication, and consensus. Decision making and compromise, while not guaranteed, seems easier with a team of two than five or six.
5. Two-person teams help break down the separate-subject instructional approach. With this approach, teachers naturally think beyond single subjects. Instruction focuses on the content and skills that students need to complete the task at hand.

In previous years, teaching on four- or five-teacher teams had been an unsatisfying experience for us. There was little time available to address student needs. Engaging students in classroom decisions and curriculum development was virtually impossible. We felt that in order to make school experiences relevant, we had to know our students well. Having only 58 students meant having more time to understand and work with our students.

The smaller team size facilitated more use of alternative assessments. We were able to effectively evaluate portfolios from our 58 students, which would have been impossible on a team of 120 or more. Because academic rigor was important, all writings submitted from our students were graded thoroughly for mechanics, grammar, and content. We also incorporated a redo policy that enabled students to improve their work. This would not have been feasible if our team size had been larger.

Learning outside the confines of the classroom was not a problem for our team. Having only 58 students permitted us to organize field trips using only one large bus. We were able to schedule research time in our media center more easily. This allowed our whole team to work on research at the same time.

Having a smaller group of students enabled us to utilize lunch time as work time. If students were involved in their projects and did not want lunch to interrupt their concentration, we sent a note down to the lunchroom to let our lunchroom manager know that we would be eating in our classrooms.

Having a two-teacher team allowed us the opportunity to call team meetings as needed. Our schedule was flexible enough that we would just stop what we were doing and gather for team discussions. Getting together with only our two classes was not as disruptive as it would have been on a larger team. Group discussions were more effective with a small team than with a larger group. In one of our team meetings, we asked our students how their eighth-grade year was different from their sixth- and seventh-grade years. Some students responded:

- My eighth-grade educational experience has been different from sixth and seventh because I only have two teachers, we work more in groups, and a whole lot less book work, we went on more field trips.
- It is just different. When we were in 6th & 7th grade we had 4 teacher [sic], now we only have two. All our subject [sic] were seperate, now there [sic] combined.
- It is nice because you don't have to go to the individual classes and all of them are blended into one.
- [I learned a lot] By knowing where everything is located and knowing all the teachers.
- I like it better because we don't have to change classes. I have learned more in eighth grade, in my half a year, than my whole 6th & 7th grade year put together. I have learned more about other people this year. I feel that integrated curriculum is more effective on me rather than split-up classes. We get to do more hands-on activities in integrated curriculum.

Some students felt that increasing the number of teachers they had was synonymous with getting older or growing up. In the beginning, they viewed two-teacher teams as a "regression" to sixth-grade days. We pointed out the benefits of being able to spend more time completing tasks rather than stopping just because it was time to change classes. We were able to go on more field trips and do more creative assessments.

## TEAM TEACHING

Another benefit of having a smaller team was team teaching. To us, team teaching meant working together—at the same time—with our team of students. Together with our students we planned topics, determined content, set goals, and created assessment tools for use in evaluation. During the initial planning session for our Human Interactions and the Environment unit, we were all together in one classroom. As students brainstormed environmental concerns, Elaine wrote down their ideas on an overhead projector. On another overhead, Karen wrote what content and skills our students said they needed to learn. The two lists were then combined to ensure that appropriate content and skills were incorporated into each group's project.

To facilitate project work, we sometimes divided the team. One of us would have an instructional activity in one room, while the other would be conducting a different activity in the other room. We would then swap students to continue the lessons. An example of this arrangement was during the Leadership unit. Students separated into two skills classes. Elaine worked with one group on topography and general map skills while Karen worked with the other group on paleontology labs.

## CLASS SCHEDULES

Block scheduling helped meet our needs. The McHome Team schedule was as follows:

| | |
|---|---|
| 7:30–7:40 | Homeroom (attendance and announcements) |
| 7:45–8:35 | Math |
| 8:35–9:30 | Exploratory A |
| 9:30–10:30 | Exploratory B |
| 10:30–10:35 | Locker/Restroom Break |
| 10:35–2:15 | Block Time (30-minute lunch included) |

One of the main benefits from this type of scheduling was flexibility in the block time. Sometimes in order to facilitate group project work, our students needed skills classes to gain basic knowledge about their topics. During the Human Migrations unit, for example, in order for our students to complete their short stories or Nickelodeons about their families' migration to America, we taught separate classes on map skills and ocean currents and wind currents. Next we had project work time followed by team group processing. This last part of the day was used to review the day's work, help answer questions related to project work or any group problems, and set the next day's agenda.

We had to take into consideration our ESL (English as a Second Language) students when planning schedules. Our ESL students were pulled during part of one exploratory class and about 20 minutes at the beginning of our block time. Having students in a pull-out program is an obstacle that must be addressed when planning a large period of block time. We arranged for our ESL students to be briefed by a student as soon as they came back to our team. This way they were soon caught up and were able to actively participate.

Having no rigid bell schedule during our block time had both its advantages and disadvantages. It took a while for students to "retrain" themselves since they were used to changing classes every 45 minutes. Eventually our students were able to concentrate and work for longer periods of uninterrupted time. During one of our group processing sessions, we discussed this issue with them. It was decided that we needed to take breaks and stretch a while to break up long periods of block time.

## CLASSROOM ORGANIZATION

The McHome Team year was a challenge due to the physical setting of our classrooms. In our initial McHome Team proposal we had requested connecting rooms with a movable center wall. When we got our room assignments, however, we were not connected or even side-by-side. Our classrooms were placed across the hall from one another. To accommodate team teaching, team planning, and project work, we often met in one classroom.

To allow the entire team to gather at one time, we sometimes arranged the team in two groups, facing each other. With this arrangement, students could interact with each other and also see the chalkboard. This physical setting was most commonly used for initial unit development. When conducting group processing sessions, we often sat on the floor in a circle. This less formal arrangement helped facilitate discussion.

Sometimes we needed to get the whole team together but have them seated with their project group members. We pulled extra tables and chairs into Karen's room (which was a slightly bigger lab classroom). Such an arrangement was used for an environmental conference our team held during the Human Interactions and the Environment unit. Students worked in groups to complete labs, generate group-designed research questions, learn more about the environment of Georgia, and engage in other various environmental awareness activities.

When the groups were working on their projects, we operated under an "open classroom" setting where both rooms were used. During the Human and Civil Rights and Responsibilities unit, groups could be found in both rooms writing scripts and creating scenery for their play. Students needed all of the space that was available and asked if we could set up temporary teacher desks out in the hall. This arrangement allowed us to monitor both classrooms from our hall location.

## CONCLUSION

Flexible scheduling of our time and organizational structures (such as our two-teacher team) allowed us to gain a better understanding of our students' personalities, interests, learning styles, and abilities. This understanding helped us in developing a coherent curriculum—one that was responsive to the needs of our students.

On Friday we will take this opportunity to teach relevant geography (South Florida/Louisiana) and earth science (hurricanes) content and, of course, our first unit, Human Migration, falls into place. Where will these people go? Will people migrate to these areas because of jobs created by the rebuilding efforts? (We are having so much fun!)

*[FRIDAY, 8/28/92]*
We had about eight students come in early. One student came in with her dad and brought two huge bags of clothes. Between our classes and others, we collected 16 boxes of assorted items. The connection has been made between talking about being an Involved Citizen and really being one.

To make sure students understood the adult roles, they prepared skits (two per group). We spent $1^1/_2$ hours filming them. This was their first performance-based assessment. Those who don't like their grade will be given an opportunity to do an alternative assessment.

I have been thinking. We have been confused ourselves. Involved Citizen, Collaborative Contributor, etc., are not adult roles … they involve skills that prepare you for your adult roles of worker, family member, life-long learner, participating citizen, etc. We will have to correct this on Monday.

After grading their first written assignment (Letter to Parents), I realize we have much work to do. Maybe these kids don't know what excellence looks like. They will be able to redo the assignment.

**HOW?**

Reflections on our first week helped us to think more deeply about our curriculum. We realized, even after only one week of school, we needed to constantly check ourselves to see that we were integrating the curriculum, explicitly making connections with the students about the curriculum, clarifying terminology with our students, finding ways to show our students what excellence looks like, and finding ways to make learning relevant and fun.

## Example 2

**WHAT?**

*Student Journal.* Students were asked to write in a journal their impressions of the first week on the McHome Team. They were asked to respond to these questions: How is this team different? What do I like about this team? What do I not like about this team?

**WHEN?**

8/31/92, First Week of School

**WHO?**

McHome Team Students

**WHERE?**

Classroom

**WHY?**

We had done a lot that was different the first week of school: we didn't issue textbooks, we didn't have traditional classes, and we didn't assign homework. We (students and teachers) needed to have the students clarify (in writing) their thoughts about the McHome Team.

*[JOURNAL 1, 8/31/92]*
My first impressions of the McHome Team was boring, stupid, mean teachers. Then as the days went on in school I found out different. The teachers were nicer, and it was great. I like the people on this team. I like the teachers and the things we do. We have fun on this team. Our teachers are taking us on a field trip Thursday. That is so cool and so soon. What I don't like about the team is the way we don't change classes cause [sic] it makes the day longer and boring and some of the things that we do are boring and I think that is it. But if you ask me I think we are going to have a pretty cool year.

*[JOURNAL 2, 8/31/92]*
Let me see. My first impressions of the McHome team the first week of school. I had been told that we would be working with groups. That's good for me because I am on a totally different team from last year. Anyway, my first impression will probaly [sic] last because I don't think I have ever thought so much that first week. I felt uncomfortable at first, but then I got used to it.

　　This team is different from any other that I have been on because we got to make our own rules. We got to work in groups and get to know one another better.

　　I like this team because I can say what I feel and people will listen to me. They may laugh, but I know that they listened.

　　I don't like this team because ... well, I don't have any reasons not to like this team.

I like the fact that we get to go on more feildtrips [sic] than last year, also!

*[JOURNAL 3, 8/31/92]*

This team is different in a lot of ways. The way we came up with our rules for the year. We came up with ideas ourselves for what we wanted our rules to be. I also think the name is different but I like it.

The teachers are nice. I like the way she lets us work in groups a lot. I can also see that the teachers agree on pretty much the same things. They also have a sense of humor but can be strict when they need to be.

The things I don't like was [sic] that on the 1st week or few days it got boring after a while and we weren't really able to think. The teachers got restless and so did we. It would have been better if we could have rested from it and then went back to it with a fresh way of thinking. I noticed that at first people were fresh and wanted to talk and then it got sort of boring.

## HOW?

These three student journal entries are representative of the McHome Team students. The reflections of the students were invaluable to us because they gave us a glimpse into our students' thoughts. The students stated they liked being on the McHome Team and that it was "different." They didn't like the long discussions that were necessary to set up the Team Management Plan and Group Guidelines. Because we knew how our students felt, we were able to address their concerns right away. We had a team meeting where we discussed the advantages, disadvantages, and importance of taking the time to set up a democratic classroom.

## Example 3

### WHAT?

*Student Journal.* Students were asked to reflect in their journals on their first 3 weeks, their next 3 weeks, and connections they had made.

### WHEN?

9/11/92, Human Migration unit

### WHO?

McHome Team Students

**WHERE?**

Classroom

**WHY?**

Making connections between school and the outside world was one of our long-term McHome Team goals. During the first 2 weeks of the Human Migration unit, we had in-depth large-group discussions about the following: why the students lived in Duluth, Georgia, where their ancestors came from, and why they migrated (see Chapter 5). We wanted our students to reflect on their first 3 weeks of school to see if any connections had been made.

> *[JOURNAL 1, 9/11/92]*
> My first 3 weeks were good. I had lots of fun. I realized this team wasn't going to be a "free ride." I admit at first I thought this was going to be easy, we weren't doing much except for sitting and talking. Now I know differently. Looking up my ancestors and doing my report on South Africa told me that this wasn't going to be a "free ride." I'm glad because I like challenges. The next 3 weeks are looking good. I think this Nickelodeon is going to [be] really neat and fun. I love to be creative. So it works out. Well for me I think it's going to be an excellent year.

> *[JOURNAL 2, 9/11/92]*
> Our first three weeks have been about getting to know each other. It made me come up with what a good teacher is and what a good student is. The Human Migration unit is helping me find out information about my ancestors. I am also finding out about what is going on in different countries and what effects it has on me.
> Our next three weeks are going to be about more Human Migration. We get to do a Nickelodeon which is connected to me because I use my history to create it. I will also have to make a family tree of my relatives. I look forward to studying this subject. I just hope I don't have a hard time.

> *[JOURNAL 3, 9/11/92]*
> The first three weeks I think that the activities connected to me because what we did was make our classroom rules and guidelines and that definitely connects to me because I have to follow them. I will be affected if I do not follow them because we also made consequesces [sic].

The next three weeks will affect me because we are learning about our ancestors and how they got here and why they came. And if they hadn't come I would not be here. We're also going to learn about our state (Georgia) & how & why it was founded & that effects [sic] me because I also would not be here if it was not founded.

## HOW?

These three student journal entries are representative of the McHome Team students. It was clear to us all (students and teachers) that connections had been made. Thus, we didn't have to stop and group process.

## Example 4

### WHAT?

*Student Journal.* Students were asked to reflect in their journals on their research progress, materials for their assessments (e.g., Nickelodeon and research papers), and their successes.

### WHEN?

9/16/92, Human Migration unit

### WHO?

McHome Team Students

### WHERE?

Classroom

### WHY?

This reflection took place approximately 2 weeks before the end of the Human Migration unit. The students had accepted quite a bit of personal responsibility for their own learning at this point. We wanted to see if our students understood the curriculum and how they felt about their work.

> *[JOURNAL 1, 9/16/92]*
> So far I think I'm doing OK, all except for the interview. I turned it in a little late. And also I didn't have enough bibliography, but I fixed that problem very fast.
>     I think that the Nickelodeon will be very fun. I have done a project very similar to this one, but I think this one will turn out different.

My success this year has turned out great. I have gotten everything signed that I was supposed to. I am trying very hard to follow all of the guidelines. But even if I break one of the guidelines I have my teachers behind me helping me.

*[JOURNAL 2, 9/16/92]*

I think I have made excellent progress on my research paper. At first I got off on a slow start. I was worried I wouldn't finish on time, but now I'm not worried because the hard part is done. The hard part was the research. I had some trouble on some questions, but on most of them I found easily [sic].

For our Nickelodeon I need to get everything except paper. I'm having trouble finding a good big box. Also I can't find any rolls to make a projector.

I think I have been very successful this year. I have turned in everything on time and gotten good grades.

*[JOURNAL 3, 9/16/92]*

I feel that I am pretty organized in the progress in my reasearch [sic] paper. I have already turned in everything that has been due on time. I need to write my report & make the map and I'll be done the final copy of them [sic].

For the Nickloden [sic] I need to bring in paper towel rolls (tubes) & white paper 8 1/2 x 11 and it needs to be computer paper. I need a box so the scene will be visible. And I need bold colors or outline it in black. Outside the box cover with paper/or fabric, paine [sic], or solid contact paper. I need more than 14 frames.

I think that my year so far has been successful. I feel that the success plan has really helped me.

**HOW?**

This reflection was used as a form of self-assessment. Students used this reflection as a checklist: what I understand about the project, what I have done up until now, and what I still have to do. They also used this reflection as a way of acknowledging and celebrating their successes.

We (teachers) also used the reflections as a form of assessment. As we read the reflections we mentally made note of which students had their projects under control and who needed assistance. Student successes were acknowledgment that our curriculum was addressing our goals: students were developing a deeper understanding of content, accepting responsibilities, taking risks, and having fun.

## Example 5

**WHAT?**

*Student Journal.* Students were asked to reflect on the following: what I liked and didn't like about the first 6 weeks and what to do about it.

**WHEN?**

10/6/92, Human Migration unit

**WHO?**

McHome Team Students

**WHERE?**

Classroom

**WHY?**

This was the end of the first 6 weeks on the McHome Team. We had developed the McHome Team Management Plan, established group norms, set group-work guidelines, revised grading criteria, and codeveloped curriculum. We wanted to stop and reflect on what we had accomplished and what still needed to be done.

> *[JOURNAL 1, 10/6/92]*
> I liked the first 6 weeks because we kinda made up the rules and guidelines. I like finding out where my ansetors [sic] came from and why they left. I like finding out about other countries and what it happining [sic] there. My favorite thing we did this 6 weeks in drawing thing like the Nickalodian [sic] and the family sheald [sic].
>
> What I didn't like about the first 6 weeks was the warnings. They killed me. I'm not good about turning in things on time but the warnings helped me a little bit.
>
> The way I would do it is to not have wornings [sic] for not turning in things and only have warnings for everything else. Also I would change the conciqunes [sic] of the warning like making the 9th warning an extra assignment and then everything else the same.

> *[JOURNAL 2, 10/6/92]*
> I liked working in group because we were able to take an idea and take another one and make just one idea. I also liked the way we were able as the stadents [sic] to make decisions involving the way we felt.

I didn't like the way our grading was done. I also didn't like taking so many notes in one day.

I think that the first six weeks were a pretty good way to start the year off. I felt that we are able to be good students and by the way, we have a say-so on everything, we should have good grades. But I would like to have a little more activities out of the classroom.

*[JOURNAL 3, 10/6/92]*
I liked a lot about the first 6 weeks. We got to pick our own rules. We got to sit by anybody we wanted too [sic]. I liked we had no books. I liked having break.

I didn't like have [sic] only one class. I didn't like having to write a plan for everything we do. I didn't like that we have to go from room to room everyday!

I would pick one classroom for us to stay in everyday and don't move from classroom to classroom everyday.

**HOW?**

These reflections were very informative. They presented clear dichotomies. Some students stated that they liked having responsibilities whereas others felt overwhelmed by the demanding tasks they had set for themselves. Some students liked the whole team moving from Karen's class to Elaine's class whereas other students wanted to stay in one room or the other. Some students liked setting up our democratic classroom whereas others complained that it took too much time. Some students perceived they were not having much homework whereas others perceived they had too much. Some students wanted more project work whereas others wanted less.

The reflections were shared with the team. As a team, we discussed and debated these issues. We all realized that because there were 60 students and two teachers on the McHome Team, coming to a complete consensus was not always possible. What was important, however, was the understanding that we (the team) would always take the time to address the issues and concerns of everyone.

## Example 6

**WHAT?**

*Individual and Group Interviews.* Individuals and groups of students were asked to reflect on their project work: What are you working on? What have you done to answer this question? How are you being taught this year in relation to your previous education?

**WHEN?**

11/13/92, Human Interactions unit

**WHO?**

McHome Team Students

**WHERE?**

The students were interviewed wherever they were working in the school at that time: in the hall, in the media center, in the classroom.

**WHY?**

We wanted to get the students' perspectives regarding the curriculum. Individuals and groups of students were asked to reflect on their current projects.

The following is an example of one interview:

> *What are you working on?* "Child abuse related to drugs."
> *What have you done to answer your question?* "I brainstormed, narrowed the list. I could do something about it. I have overheads with facts, a video of how it might look, and ways to notice it and prevent it, and a poster."
> *How are you being taught this year in relationship to your previous education?* "We get to be ourselves. We work in groups or as individuals. There is not just one grade. It is more real life. We get to work with other people. We learn from other students when they make presentations, etc. I have learned how to use the Macintosh computer, how to write letters better, how to conduct good interviews, prepare surveys, and use SIRS [Social Issues Resource Service]."

**HOW?**

These interviews were affirmation that our students were personally engaged in coherent curriculum. We shared the interview transcripts with parents to help them better understand our McHome Team curriculum.

## Example 7

**WHAT?**

*Student Questionnaire.* Students were asked to reflect on their second 6 weeks using the following questions:

1. What do you like the most about our democratic classroom?
2. What do you like least about our democratic classroom?
3. What do you like about designing your own project?
4. What do you not like about designing your own project?
5. What support (activities, skills, printed information) was helpful in accomplishing your goals?
6. If you had a problem working in your group and your group identified that problem, explain the problem and the process your group used to solve it.
7. If you had a problem the group did not solve, explain the problem and explain why the group did not solve it.
8. If your group did not have a problem working together, explain your success.

**WHEN?**

11/24/92, Human Interactions unit

**WHO?**

McHome Team Students

**WHERE?**

Classroom

**WHY?**

We had just finished the second unit of the year, Human Interactions. During this unit the students were heavily involved in democratic processes in designing their own projects. They had worked for an entire grading period with the same interest group. The following are two randomly selected female and male reflections:

1. What do you like the most about our democratic classroom?
   *Female student:* I enjoyed having this kind of class. The teachers didn't tell us what to do, I liked that! I think it becomes more interesting like that.
   *Male student:* The way we vote, the majority rule went my way every time. That's why I like it.

2. What do you like least about our democratic classroom?
   *Female student:* Sometimes it was hard since the teachers didn't tell us what to do. Because we're used to teachers telling us what to do, so sometimes we could get lost.

*Male student:* The way some people drag things on & on about why they don't want things after everyone has voted.

3. What do you like about designing your own project?
   *Female student:* Well, I liked picking our project, but I think we should be able to pick the broad topic to [sic].
   *Male student:* If you design your own project it should insure [sic] you an A.

4. What do you not like about designing your own project?
   *Female student:* I didn't like having so many smaller choices.
   *Male student:* I dislike all the effort we have to put into it because it seems like 24 hours a day I am doing schoolwork.

5. What support (activities, skills, printed information) was helpful in accomplishing your goals?
   *Female student:* We got handouts that helped us on our presentation.
   *Male student:* The deadline to finish because it made you work twice as hard as you would have.

6. If you had a problem working in your group, and your group identified that problem, explain that problem and the process your group used to solve it.
   *Female student:* No problem.
   *Male student:* We made a plan of action and we all stated our opinions on paper and read them and promised each other we wouldn't do what we had done in the past.

7. If you had a problem the group did not solve, explain the problem and explain why the group did not solve it.
   *Female student:* No problem.
   *Male student:* We didn't. Two of the people in our group wined [sic] & complained because they didn't get along, so we let them in temporary to see how it would work out, and we didn't like it and they wouldn't leave our group and were trying to take credit for work we did. One complains for every little thing. We didn't want them so he told the teacher he was in our group and she made us keep them.

8. If your group did not have a problem working together, explain your success.
   *Female student:* Well, I think our group worked well together. Because we all thought kinda alike and we worked good together. So I think that's what made us successful.

> *Male student:* We really didn't have a problem giving work and
> doing it with the group except complaining that got on my
> nerves.

**HOW?**

In these reflections, our students revealed their interest in being more
involved in curriculum development. These reflections helped the team in
conceptualizing the next thematic unit, Human Interactions and the
Environment.

These reflections also proved to be useful in that they were a way for
students to vent frustrations. We personally acknowledged their frustrations
by providing written feedback to each student.

## Example 8

**WHAT?**

*Quiz.* Students were asked to reflect and to respond to the following questions:

1. List the countries of the Middle East and North Africa (bordering
   the Mediterranean Sea).
2. Draw and label the main parts of a plant cell and animal cell.

**WHEN?**

11/24/92, Human Interactions unit

**WHO?**

McHome Team Students

**WHERE?**

Classroom

**WHY?**

After about 18 weeks of integrated curriculum, our students told us they
felt they weren't learning enough facts and figures from textbooks. They said
they felt they learned more the traditional way, "like in sixth and seventh
grades." So, during lunch that day, we went to the seventh-grade teachers
to find out what main concepts our students had been taught in science and
social studies. The teachers told us they had studied plant and animal cells

and the geography and culture of the Middle East. After lunch, we told our students they were going to have a quiz. When they complained, we replied:

> Oh, you know the information. You studied this last year. Get out a piece of paper, and put your name at the top. On the front of the paper, list the countries of the Middle East and North Africa bordering the Mediterranean Sea. Don't worry, you don't have to name the capitals or their GNP, even though we know you studied that last year. Then, on the back, draw and label the main parts of a plant cell and an animal cell. Don't worry about naming the functions of each part.

For 10 minutes, our students sweated and squirmed. No one passed the quiz (see Figures 9.1a, 9.1b, and 9.1c).

We asked the students, "Since you spent most of your seventh-grade school year studying these facts through a traditional approach to teaching and learning, and you still haven't learned them, what was the point?" One student replied, "Yeah, if I want to know about the rivers of Africa, I can look them up in an atlas." "Right," we agreed, "you need to learn *how* to learn, not just memorize the facts."

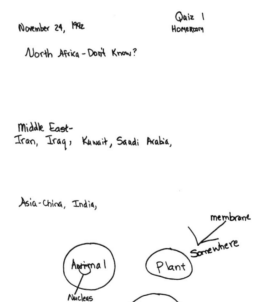

**Student a**

**Figure 9.1a–c.** Student quizzes.

November 24, 1992

North Africa
Middle East
Iran
Belgium
Iseral
Saudi Aradi

Asia
?

**Student b**   plant cell     animal cell

North Africa, Middle East, Asia

North Africa

?

Middle east
Iraq
Iran
Kuatt

Aisa

?

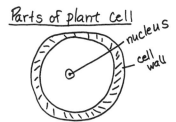

Parts of plant cell

nucleus

cell wall

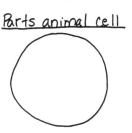

Parts animal cell

**Student c**

**HOW?**

What followed was an in-depth discussion of how their learning this year was different from other school years. This year they were learning how to learn and apply what they were learning. This reflection on the importance of what and how you learn was critical to all of us. We felt our students should understand that the various subject areas were important (they were useful in answering student-posed questions) but that they were not the focus of our curriculum (Beane, 1995a). This discussion reinforced the need for coherent curriculum.

Not long after the quiz, a parent told us during a conference that she was concerned that her child was not getting a traditional education. She thought the way her daughter was taught in seventh grade was the best way. We showed the parent her daughter's almost-blank quiz. This opened up a discussion about the need for a variety of teaching strategies to facilitate meaningful learning.

## Example 9

**WHAT?**

*Student Questionnaire.* Students were asked to reflect on the following questions:

1. Define "rubric."
2. What is a rubric used for?
3. How do your teachers design rubrics?
4. How did you (or your group) design your rubric?
5. At what point in your project work do you design a rubric?
6. How did designing your own rubric affect your project preparation?
7. How do you feel about using rubrics for assessment as opposed to traditional multiple-choice, fill-in-the-blank, true/false tests, etc.?

**WHEN?**

11/30/92, Human Interactions unit

**WHO?**

McHome Team Students

**WHERE?**

Classroom

**WHY?**

Our students designed their own rubrics for the first time during the Human Interactions unit. We wanted to find out if our students completely understood what rubrics were and how they could be utilized.

The following are two randomly selected reflections:

1. Define "rubric."
   *Female student 1:* A grade sheet showing procedure of something in order from excellent, good, not good, & not.
   *Female student 2:* Self evaluation on what you do.

2. What is a rubric used for?
   *Female student 1:* It is used to grade you by what you have planned to do and gives you something to follow as you do a project.
   *Female student 2:* It is used for grading you on what you did and didn't do.

3. How do your teachers design rubrics?
   *Female student 1:* They don't, we design them.
   *Female student 2:* They design them based upon what is acceptable for the full pts or the best grade.

4. How did you (or your group) design your rubric?
   *Female student 1:* I started at Excellent, thought of everything that would make a project excellent and then worked it down to GOOD, NOT GOOD, & NOT IT AT ALL.
   *Female student 2:* We designed it based apon [sic] what was acceptable for full pts and we based it upon what things were needed and what things we had.

5. At what point in your project work do you design a rubric?
   *Female student 1:* After you've picked topic, got connections, & made connections statement.
   *Female student 2:* At the begining [sic] because you need to know what to do and what needs to be done to get total pts.

6. How did designing your own rubric affect your project preparation?
   *Female student 1:* In my case it didn't help much but I'm sure in others it helped alot [sic] because they probably followed it and got a good grade.
   *Female student 2:* It made it easier because we decided what we needed.

7. How do you feel about using rubrics for assessment as opposed to traditional multiple choice, fill-in-the-blank, true/false tests, etc.?

   *Female student 1:* I like true/false tests better but I guess that's because it's easier and taking a free ride but I learned more skills, like following through w/what you say your [sic] gonna do w/a rubric.

   *Female student 2:* I think designing your own rubric gives you more freedom to choose what is more important to you, and which way you would like to learn more information. I didn't like how if we didn't do one thing we got a zero. I think we should get points off instead.

## HOW?

Again, this reflection was a type of assessment. We knew that our students would be using rubrics for the rest of the school year. We needed to know if they clearly understood what rubrics were for and how they were developed. What was refreshing for us as we read these reflections was that our students were accepting (sometimes willingly and sometimes not so willingly) responsibility for their decisions. And they were taking risks and learning from their mistakes.

## Example 10

### WHAT?

*Student Response Essay.* Students were asked to reflect on these questions as they wrote:

1. What is designing down?
2. What is the purpose of designing down?
3. How do you use the designing-down format?
4. How did it help your "mini" lesson?
5. Why are the topic boxes in the order they are in?
6. Why are group projects and group processing a good idea?
7. Why are group projects and group processing a bad idea?

### WHEN?

2/19/93, Human Interactions and the Environment unit

### WHO?

McHome Team Students

**WHERE?**

Classroom

**WHY?**

We had been using the designing-down format for our unit development since the Human Migration unit. This was the first time our students had personally applied this knowledge by developing their own lessons utilizing the designing-down format. In this reflection we wanted to know if our students really understood this format. We also wanted to know if the students were utilizing their group processing skills as they worked with their group members. We wanted to know if our students had internalized these processes.

The following are randomly chosen responses from two of our students:

*MALE STUDENT:*

The designing down format is almost like a Rubric. It is a guideline to show you how to do your project. I used it to help me better understand what was going to be in my project and how I was going to do it. It helped my mini lesson by showing me exactly how to do it and what was supposed to be in it. The topic boxes are in the order they are in because each evaluation follows the box before it. They are in chronological order. I think that doing a group project and using group processing is a good idea because you don't have to do every single part of it by yourself. I also think that group processing is a good idea because if you are doing a project alone, you might leave something out that you wouldn't have if you were in a group.

*FEMALE STUDENT:*

The purpose of disigning [sic] down is to help you get organized and to help yourself understand what you are doing on maybe a project or something. I used the designing down with my mini lesson on smog. And it help [sic] me and my group greatly. It help [sic] us because it told [sic] me and the group understand what we are doing step by step. On the designing down the boxes are in that order because that is what you need to know step by step. I really enjoy having the designing down. It help [sic] us a lot on our mini lesson. Thank you. I enjoy the projects and the processing a lot. Because if we didn't have the passed [sic] projects I wouldn't have been able to do this. I also enjoyed it because we got to work w/different people and see how others work w/others. I enjoyed it alot [sic] and I wanted to say thank you.

**HOW?**

We knew from these reflections that our students were ready for even more responsibility in curriculum development. These reflections also indicated that our students were learning how to work effectively with a diversity of people, which was one of our long-term goals.

## Example 11

**WHAT?**

*Student Response Essay.* Students were asked to reflect on the following questions regarding the usefulness of designing down:

> 1. How will a designing-down sheet help me in high school?
> 2. How will a designing-down sheet help me in the workplace?

**WHEN?**

3/5/93, Human/Civil Rights and Responsibilities unit

**WHO?**

McHome Team Students

**WHERE?**

Classroom

**WHY?**

We wanted to see if our students were making connections between what they were learning now on the McHome Team and their future. We specifically wanted to see if we were achieving our long-term goal of making connections between school and the outside world.

The following are examples of student response essays:

> *STUDENT 1:*
> I believe that using a designing-down form will help me in high school because I will be able to mentally picture what it is I want to do. This is also true in a work situation. I can use the form to show what I want fellow classmates or fellow employees to do. The assessment part of the designing-down form would be for when our project was complete and we wanted to evaluate what we've accomplished. I think using a designing-down form is helpful to us all.

Using it now will prepare us for future endeavors.

*STUDENT 2:*
A designing down is going to help me in high school by showing me on projects what I'm trying to tell about, how I'm going to tell about it, why I'm telling about it, and how I intend to get the information needed. This will help me because then I will no [sic] what I'm doing and will be able to research with no problems. A designing down will help me in my workplace by letting me show my boss exactly what I'm doing. It will also help me explain what I'm doing to co-workers.

*STUDENT 3:*
Using a designing-down sheet/format will help me in high school by making me more organised [sic] and letting me do better work on big projects. It can also help me on little projects. Using a designing-down sheet/format can help me in the workplace by helping me stay organised [sic]. If I was doing something that required major attention, it would help me to keep on line with the project. It can help me be sucessful [sic] in my future job no matter what it is. The designing-down sheet can help you in everyday life.

**HOW?**

The students' essays indicated to us that they were indeed making connections. They were seeing direct applications of what they were experiencing in the classroom to their future endeavors in high school and beyond. These essays also gave us additional information regarding our curriculum. As we read them, we felt elated. This was further evidence that our students were actively participating in their own learning, developing deeper understanding of content, taking risks and learning from mistakes, and learning to work effectively. These student reflections were evidence of the McHome Team's coherent curriculum!

## Example 12

**WHAT?**

*Student-Initiated Team Meeting.* Girls demanded team meeting to discuss boys' behavior in the cafeteria.

**WHEN?**

3/24/93, Leadership unit

**WHO?**

McHome Team Students and Teachers

**WHERE?**

Classroom

**WHY?**

Several of our girls expressed concern about the behavior of some our boys. The girls had observed some of the boys making rude remarks about other students in the cafeteria. For example, some of the comments included, "Boy, look at the ugly _____ on that one." "Get a load of the _____ on that girl." "Hey, can you believe how ugly that one is?" Our girls were livid! They demanded a team meeting to discuss this issue. The girls wanted to confront the boys and make them take responsibility for their behavior in front of the whole team.

While the team was having our after lunch ice cream break, these girls arranged the classroom for a team meeting. They stacked the chairs and pushed the desks against the wall so that the entire team could sit on the floor in a circle.

The girls led the team meeting. After all were seated, they began. "We asked for this meeting because we are upset about some of the boys' behavior in the cafeteria." They went on to say what they had overheard. Without calling names, the girls asked the team what they thought of this behavior. After much discussion and debate, the boys came forward, on their own, and apologized for their behavior. They assured the whole team that it would never happen again.

**HOW?**

All year our curriculum had emphasized problem-posing/problem-solving strategies. This team reflection revealed that our students had internalized these strategies. It was satisfying for all of us that the students could recognize and solve problems on their own (initiate leadership) without any help from adults. It was also encouraging that our students were accepting responsibility for their own actions.

## Example 13

**WHAT?**

*Student Questionnaire.* Students were asked to reflect on the following questions:

1. In school, how do you feel you learn best? (Provide examples and explain.)
2. What do you think the middle school curriculum should be? (What do you want to learn?)
3. What are some suggestions for improving the middle school experience for students?
4. How has your eighth-grade educational experience been different from sixth and seventh grades?
5. How do you feel about integrated curriculum (science, social studies, language arts taught together)?
6. How has your eighth-grade educational experience been the same as your sixth and seventh grades?
7. Identify and explain (as many examples as you can) things you learned this year that you think will help you in high school and beyond.

## WHEN?

4/26/93, Communities of the Future unit

## WHO?

McHome Team Students

## WHERE?

Classroom

## WHY?

Because this was the end of the school year, it was important for our students to reflect on their McHome Team year and for us (teachers) to know how they felt about this experience.

The following are randomly selected examples of student responses (ranked by ability). Teachers' perceptions of student motivation and academic ability were the determinants for the ranking. Students were ranked as having high ability (student 1), average ability (student 2), or low ability (student 3).

1. In school, how do you feel you learn best? (Provide examples and explain.)
   *Student 1:* I feel that I learn best when I am in a small group. I learned a lot in the first six weeks doing a project on racism with two of the other students in my class. I can get more

information from other people and combine it with my information and come up with a lot of information that is interesting
to me and other people.

*Student 2:* In school I feel that I learn best when teachers make
the assignments fun. When they just assign assignments that
aren't fun, I don't feel like I learn as much because when
they're fun I learn while I'm having fun, and it makes what I've
learned "stick" better. (Example: The living timeline.)

*Student 3:* I feel the best way I learn best is working in small
groups. I can get input from other people in the group. Ex)
[sic] in doing projects, the other people could give input about
what to do and ideas on how to do it.

2. What do you think the middle school curriculum should be?
(What do you want to learn?)

*Student 1:* I would like to learn more about current issues rather
than history. Current issues to me are much more interesting.

*Student 2:* I think the Middle School Curriculum is pretty good
like it is. Although I feel that since I've come to this school I've
learned more about Human/Civil Rights than I did in my other
school because instead of just teaching about it, Mis [sic]
Homestead & McGinnis gave more examples of it. For instance
talking about the Holocoust [sic], watching Roots etc. I thing
this helps you relate better to what your [sic] learning about.

*Student 3:* I think the curriculum should kinda be the same. The
teachers should just make the subjects more fun. The
exploratories should be what you want to do and not have you
get stuck with something you hate.

3. What are some suggestions for improving the middle school experience for students?

*Student 1:* 1. Learn about more current issues. 2. Learn about
more serious issues such as racism, abortion, AIDS, and drugs.

*Student 2:* To improve middle school experience teachers should
give the student a choice about how they want to learn about a
topic. (With a group, individual, oral project) I think this will
help them learn more thoroughly about what your [sic] and
have fun in the process.

*Student 3:* Some suggestions are have the teachers making the
subject fun, having work less complicated, smaller classes so
the kids can have a 1-one-1 [sic] with the teacher so the kids
can understand work better and the teacher has more attention
to 1 student, and work is more explained.

4. How has your eighth-grade educational experience been different from your sixth and seventh grades?

    *Student 1:* I have learned more in 8th grade, in my half a year, than my whole 6th & 7th grade year put together. I have learned more about other people this year.

    *Student 2:* Eighth grade has been diff. because it's been funner [sic] and I think I've learned more. Also I've had less homework.

    *Student 3:* The eigth [sic] grade differs from 6th & 7th grades because in 6th & 7th, I changed classes. In 8th, while I was here, we stayed together. That's basiclly [sic] the only difference.

5. How do you feel about integrated curriculum (science, social studies, language arts taught together)?

    *Student 1:* I feel that integrated curriculum is more effective on me rather than split-up classes. We get to do more hands-on activities in integrated curriculum.

    *Student 2:* I think it's funner [sic] altogether, but when I'm doing a certain project I don't really know what subject(s) it's gonna be graded on.

    *Student 3:* I don't like it very much. I don't know whether I'm in science, history, language arts. I like the switching classes better. It's easier for me to do.

6. How has your eighth-grade educational experience been the same as your sixth and seventh grades?

    *Student 1:* It's been the same because I've learned a lot of the same stuff, but it's mostly been different!

    *Student 2:* I have been working with basically the same people every year of Middle School, so I know a lot about people, and I can understand them better.

    *Student 3:* The 8th grade has been the same as 6th & 7th is that all 3 years, I got to work in pairs and groups.

7. Identify and explain (as many examples as you can) things you learned this year that you think will help you in high school and beyond.

    *Student 1:* I have learned how to do a designing-down sheet. I want to be a lawyer, so I think that it will help me and my cases be more organized.

    *Student 2:* How to work in groups. How to work fast to get something done—explain things to class—make assignments fun.

    *Student 3:* I think I have learned *some* things to help me in high school and beyond. Learned to work well in groups. Later, I'll have to work with other people and get along. If I don't, I could either get bad grades in school or lose my job.

**HOW?**

These reflections provided our students with an opportunity to stop and look back. They reflected on what worked, what didn't work, what they learned, what connections they had made, and what they would have done differently. Again, these reflections confirmed how coherent our curriculum had become.

## Example 14

**WHAT?**

*Teacher Discussion.* Teachers wished to reflect on their year and what they had accomplished.

**WHEN?**

7/7/93–7/8/93, the End of the Year

**WHO?**

Karen, Elaine, and Elizabeth

**WHERE?**

Lake Sinclair, Georgia

**WHY?**

We knew we had experienced something remarkable during our McHome Team year. We knew our curriculum had been responsive to the interests and needs of our students while maintaining academically challenging standards. We had realized our long-term goals. We knew that we wanted to reflect on our year.

**HOW?**

This reflection helped us further conceptualize our thinking. We began this reflection by restating our philosophy of education. We also talked about the different thematic units that were codeveloped with our students, our McHome Team victories, and the obstacles we had encountered.

Our original intent, for the McHome Team year, was to integrate the curriculum. By the end of the year we knew we had accomplished much more—*our curriculum had become coherent.* We spent most of our reflection time identifying and describing what we thought were the essential components that had made *our* curriculum coherent.

We developed a chart to organize our thoughts. The chart included the components and their descriptions. We then refined this chart and came up with our *Essential Components of a Coherent Curriculum:*

- Goals
- Democratic Classroom
- Traditional and Alternative Assessments
- Content Integration
- Pedagogy
- Communication
- Scheduling and Organizational Structures
- Reflection

We realized that although we had listed them separately, these components were in fact intertwined.

## CONCLUSION

Reflecting on the McHome Team meant thinking about what had transpired. We reflected on curriculum, assessment, perceptions, connections, successes, projects, democracy, and the meaning of coherent curriculum. We utilized a variety of formats (e.g., surveys, questionnaires, journals, small- and large-group discussions). Each reflection was elicited for a different purpose.

Written student reflections were read by us (teachers). We sorted and discussed them according to issues and concerns. If there was no need for clarification, discussion, or resolution, we would not have a meeting. If there was a need, we met as a team, small group, or with individual students. These meetings helped alleviate concerns, resolve conflicts, and promote clear and open communication.

Reflecting helped us find out if we were understanding each other. Reflections also helped us see if we were addressing our goals (see Chapter 2). Sometimes we wanted to find out if our students were making connections (between our work at school and the outside world), and sometimes we wanted to find out if our students had concerns they just weren't willing to verbalize. We asked them to be specific and give suggestions for change. Through our reflections, misunderstandings were clarified, trust was reinforced, and democracy and collegiality were strengthened.

# Chapter 10

# COMMUNITIES
# OF THE FUTURE

The final unit during our quest for coherent curriculum was Communities of the Future. This unit was developed because of student concern (for their surroundings and future living conditions) and school-mandated curriculum requirements. The Communities of the Future unit, as a culminating event, provided our students with opportunities to take a more active role in the continuing development of our coherent curriculum.

In this chapter we share how the Communities of the Future unit was developed by the McHome Team. We have divided this chapter into four timeline segments: Initial Unit Preparation, Content Instruction, Determining Communities, and Development and Presentation of Communities. Portions of journals kept by students and teachers as well as student work samples are included to provide insight into the unit's development.

Each of our previous units had contributed to our understanding of coherent curriculum. The first unit, Human Migration, was designed primarily by us (teachers). We wanted to make sure we could teach content within a theme, find out if the focus of social studies would work, model integrated curriculum for our students, and have something planned to begin the school year.

The second unit, Human Interactions, was codeveloped by students and teachers. Each group of students chose a social/political issue to study. The students developed their own projects with our help and guidance. The third unit, Human Interactions and the Environment, was a Human Interactions spin-off unit. Our students were so interested in their study of social issues that affected them that they asked to continue their studies to include environmental issues of personal concern. In this unit our students took an even greater role in curriculum design.

The fourth unit, Human and Civil Rights and Responsibilities, was again codeveloped by students and teachers. During this unit, however, our students went far beyond what we had envisioned at the beginning of the unit. They were mentally and emotionally engaged as they were creating coherent curriculum.

The first four units were developed over a 6-month time period. We all were exhausted. We decided to truly work on developing coherent curriculum by being responsive to the needs and concerns of our students. They were enthusiastic about reading *Jurassic Park,* so we looked at how a leadership study could be incorporated into a novel study for our fifth unit: Leadership.

Our final unit was developed for a variety of reasons. First, since it was our culminating unit, we wanted to tie everything together. We had been collaborating with our students over the entire school year; it was time for them to take an even more active role in curriculum development. We wanted them to use skills and content knowledge they had acquired and developed over the course of the year.

Second, we knew that we had not yet covered all of the eighth-grade school-mandated curriculum. Therefore, the unit also needed to address required content (e.g., governmental and economic systems, astronomy).

Third, we wanted this unit to include all our long-term McHome Team goals. We wanted to do the following: develop a curriculum that gives students and teachers a deeper understanding of content, make connections between the school and the outside world, guide students in the learning process, encourage students to accept responsibilities, help students learn to work effectively with a diversity of people, encourage students to take risks and learn from mistakes, assist students in becoming effective problem solvers, and enable students to discover that learning can be fun.

Fourth, and finally, we wanted the last unit to be interesting and motivating for our students. This was the end of their eighth-grade school year. They were tired. They were eager to go on to high school. We knew there would be many classroom interruptions.

## INITIAL UNIT PREPARATION

In preparation for our sixth and final unit, one of the first things we did was develop a "to do" list. We brainstormed everything we knew must be addressed in the unit. We constantly referred to this list during the development of the unit:

1. Brainstorm with class past topics, skills learned, designing needed, lessons/assessments, etc.
2. Explain purpose of this *last* upcoming unit. (There's a place for teacher/student collaboration: "We know you're ready to demonstrate all we've learned this year through this upcoming unit.")
3. Explain that the students will be writing a curriculum unit for our next year's students. Brainstorm ideas for this unit based on teacher-guided questions.
4. Choose type of project (colonize space, space station, a city).
5. Create your own essential question.
6. Select skills to demonstrate.
7. Connect skills with essential question.
8. Create performance assessment to demonstrate connection statement for the unit.
9. List skills, facts, and activities needed in order to have the knowledge for the performance assessment.

The skills addressed in the unit were ones we had worked on all year. These included research skills (e.g., develop good research questions, use a variety of sources to locate information, interpret and synthesize information from a variety of media, write to communicate information). They also included technical skills (e.g., utilizing word processing, developing scaled drawings) and skills necessary to work effectively with others (e.g., cooperating, listening, contributing ideas, sharing, summarizing, checking for understanding, keeping on task, compromising, encouraging others). In addition, we also addressed organizational skills (e.g., organizing, keeping neat records, developing plans, evaluating plans, revising plans, using time wisely).

We wanted to encourage our students to use skills they had previously learned as well as focus on the following skills groups:

*Skills Group 1:* recognize problems and opportunities; devise, implement, evaluate, and revise (if necessary) a daily plan of action
*Skills Group 2:* cooperate effectively in a group setting by generating and contributing ideas through negotiation, teamwork, and leadership
*Skills Group 3:* write to communicate personal feelings, attitudes, and ideas
*Skills Group 4:* imagine, generate, and produce new ideas, solutions, or products

These skills were the basis for student assessment in this unit. The first three assessed processes while the fourth assessed product. Skills Group 1 required students to come up with some kind of a plan for group work. Skills Group 2 required students to cooperate and contribute to group work. Skills Group 3 required students to practice reflective thinking. Skills Group 4 required students to generate a product of some kind.

## CONTENT INSTRUCTION

To introduce this unit, we had a team meeting. We began the meeting by reviewing past units. We also discussed the school curriculum content we still needed to learn. We then shared our ideas for the last unit: a unit in which students would have the opportunity to examine their attitudes and values regarding society, think about what kind of community they live in now, and then create their ideal community.

One of the first things we did was to divide the team into two groups for content instruction. Elaine took one group for instruction on governmental and economic systems while Karen took the other for instruction on astronomy.

Because each community of the future group would be required to include a governmental and economic system and state the reasons for their choices, background information was needed. Choosing the right system for their community of the future was an important component of this unit. Because the governmental and economic systems of a society reflect the attitudes and values of its people, it was very important that each group member have a personal opinion as to the right system for his or her community.

Information packets on governmental and economic systems were prepared for students. The governmental systems included were monarchy, oligarchy, democracy, and dictatorship. The economic systems included were capitalism and socialism. The information packets contained definitions and examples. A list of questions was given to students to guide them in comparing governments and economic systems.

We then discussed these questions, as a class, and clarified any misconceptions and ambiguities. In small groups, students completed the Comparative Governments data retrieval chart. On the reverse side of their chart students wrote what they thought were the advantages and disadvantages of each form of government. After completing this activity, they shared their responses with the class.

Students also used information in the packet to gain a working knowledge of economic systems. We developed a list of advantages and disadvantages for capitalism and socialism and discussed them at length. Students were asked to choose which form of governmental and economic system they thought worked best together and then tell why, based on their own attitudes and values.

During the content instruction phase of the Communities of the Future unit, Elaine kept a daily journal. In the journal she stated information provided to the students, rationalized for herself the learning processes and strategies utilized, and reflected on classroom activity. The following is an excerpt from Elaine's journal:

## Thursday, April 22

*WHAT AND WHY*

Today I began the backgrounder for our final unit. Because each "Community of the Future" group will be required to choose a government and economic system and state the reasons why, background info was needed on the types of governments and economic systems.

I typed and distributed a short summary of facts about monarchy, dictatorship, oligarchy and democracy. To help the students focus on what was important to understand about the different forms of governments, I prepared an advance organizer: questions to be answered.

- Why do we need government?
- What power do governments have?
- Who governs?

The class brainstormed reasons for (1) why we need government: to organize society, to control society, to ensure the rights of citizens, to ensure safety and security, and to make money; (2) power of governments: make and enforce laws, take money (taxes), change laws, control family growth (China), imprison, take property (imminent domain); (3) who governs: elected representatives, king or queen, group of people, dictator.

I developed a data-retrieval chart for the four forms of government: monarchy, dictatorship, oligarchy, and democracy. For each form of government, each student had to answer the following questions: Who holds the power? How does the leadership change? What are the rights of the people (how do they participate in the government)?

We reviewed the three branches of our government and the checks and balances.

Because it is very important that they realize why our constitution was written, I am requiring all students to memorize the preamble of the constitution. They will be required to write a constitution for their Community of the Future.

It was evident, as we discussed the different forms of government, that they had not thought much about why we have government and what role government plays in our lives. So I adjusted the lesson to include the advantages and disadvantages of each form of government. They will be required to decide upon the best form of government for their "Community," so it is very important that each student think carefully about what form of government she would have and why.

*Reflection*

Because the students know so much about our republican form of government, it won't be necessary to spend any more class time on background info. They know enough to be able to choose a form of government for their "Community" and justify it. We will review tomorrow the advantages and disadvantages of each form of government so they will be able to choose their form of government more intelligently.

## Friday, April 23

WHAT AND WHY

Today I had the students read background info on capitalism and socialism. We discussed the following:

- Why do societies develop economic systems? Because resources are scarce and choices must be made as to the following: what to produce, how to produce it, and for whom to produce.
- What determines the form of the economic system the society chooses? The society's basic values, e.g., individual over group.

For each economic system (capitalism/socialism) I had them answer the following:

- Who owns the resources?
- Who decides what to produce?
- How are prices for items determined?

When all had finished, we discussed each question.

*Reflection*

We will be able on Monday to talk about the advantages and disadvantages of each system. They will then decide what governmental and economic system they would create if they were starting their own society. I decided to have them do this now instead of waiting until they formed their groups for the unit project because I wanted *each* student to have thought long and hard about this issue, to have a definite opinion as to the best choice, and to be able to defend their choice to the group.

The students were patient yet unenthusiastic about the topic of economic systems. Even though I told them we were preparing them for the final unit of the year, they were not very interested in the subject.

## Monday, April 26

Monday was spent reviewing the different forms of governments and economic systems and the advantages and disadvantages of each. Students now realize that the governments and economic systems of a society are a direct result of the values of the society. Monday the question was posed: If you could develop your ideal governmental system, what would it be? Each student answered specific questions, such as, Who holds the power? How do citizens give input? An organizational chart was then created.

In addition to understanding governmental and economic systems, school curriculum content in astronomy needed to be addressed. Karen took information from a variety of texts to prepare mini-lessons for the students. Topics for lessons included galaxies (e.g., constellations and life cycle of stars), our solar system (e.g., size, composition, motion, measurements of planets), and space technology (e.g., space travel, satellites). Students completed CLOZE passages (excerpts from the text with key terms deleted) and constructed constellation tubes (a cylinder with star groupings punched out at one end). These lessons were intended to be a brief content overview of which students needed to be aware should they choose to create their community in space. Karen also reviewed other science-related topics that might prove useful in developing their communities, including the composition of the atmosphere, climate and weather, energy, natural resources, and environmental protection.

## DETERMINING COMMUNITIES

After the governmental/economic systems and astronomy instruction, we had a team meeting to begin the process of determining communities. We began the team meeting with a brainstorming session. We asked the team the question, "What is needed for society to function?" The team came up with governmental services, communications, transportation, utilities, natural resources and environment, and goods and services. Small groups of students took each of the above and developed a concept map. These concept maps were shared to provide as many ideas as possible for students to use in developing their own community of the future.

The next question for the class was, "If you were going to establish a community in the future where would you go?" There were two specific "givens" for students to consider when answering the question: (1) the community must be completely isolated, and (2) you will never return home. The team decided that if they were to begin a new community in the future, it might be:

- Underwater/ocean
- On an island
- In a biosphere
- Underground
- On the moon
- On another planet

We discussed with the team that groups needed to be formed according to the needs and strengths of the group members. For example, some students are good organizers, some are effective problem solvers, and some are creative thinkers. We also needed to consider personal choice in community location.

Some students were upset because they thought they wouldn't be able to work with any of their friends. One student raised her hand and asked, "Could we have just one person in our group we wanna work with?" We said this was an excellent idea.

Students listed their first, second, and third community location choices. They also wrote down the names of three people with whom they wanted to work. Community groups were ultimately determined by three factors: location (island communities, underground communities, underwater communities, and communities on other planets), student strengths and needs, and friendship.

## DEVELOPMENT AND PRESENTATION OF COMMUNITIES

While up to now it may look as though this unit was all teacher directed, it wasn't. We were just providing the background information for the Communities of the Future unit development. For this unit, we felt it was important to teach the content before project work began. We did this because we had learned from other units that once students got involved in project work, they didn't want to stop to learn content. We were now ready for the next segment of the unit: development of communities.

During the next few days, we created assessments for our first three skills groups. To assess Skills Group 1 (recognize problems and opportunities; devise, implement, evaluate, and revise, if necessary, a plan of action), the team created a Daily Group Plan sheet (see Chapter 4). This planning format provided each group with an organized way to guide each day's work.

Elaine's journal entries give a teacher's perspective on what was happening in the classroom and the decision-making processes.

### THURSDAY, APRIL 29

To ensure student input in decisions, we asked students to give help brainstorming ideas to monitor planning of each day. We came up with a form that would help each group develop a good plan to thoughtfully prepare for the day's activities. This form is our Daily Group Plan. Karen and I worked on it after school. We made a sample plan that would help them get started in their groups.

### FRIDAY, APRIL 30

To begin class we distributed the sample Group Plan and reviewed it with the class. We decided as a class what our goals would be for the day. We began with the questions that the class brainstormed on Wednesday. Our first goal was to develop a group plan that would help answer the question: Where are we going and why?

Karen and I circulated and helped each group develop their plan for the day. Some of the groups just copied our sample plan. The day was very busy and students were on task. At the end of the day we had them get into their groups and evaluate their plans.

To demonstrate Skills Group 2 (cooperate effectively in a group setting by generating and contributing ideas through negotiation, teamwork, and leadership), the students wanted to individually assess themselves. As a team, we established the criteria for effective group work. These criteria were then used to develop the Group Evaluation Sheet (see Chapter 4).

The students elected to keep a daily journal to demonstrate Skills Group 3 (write to communicate personal feelings, attitudes, and ideas). Students reflected on their daily group activities, problems that arose, and personal feelings.

We delayed developing an assessment for Skills Group 4 (imagine, generate, and produce new ideas, solutions, or products). We decided to leave it until each group had fully researched and planned its community of the future.

Just as groups were ready to begin working on their communities, our schedule was interrupted by standardized testing; spring pictures; students registering for high school; high school peer leaders coming to talk about the high school experience; field-day sign-ups; career classes; orchestra, band, and gifted student field trips; the school play; friendship-group pictures; and the issuing of yearbooks. In addition to all of this, our eighth graders had spring fever.

In the midst of all these interruptions we began our project work. Students had their background information, their groups were formed, and they knew how they would be evaluated on the process portion of their project. We started communities development by brainstorming beginning questions:

Why are we going?
Where are we going?
What is the place like?
When are we going?
How will we select the people?
How many people are going?
What will we take?
How will we get there?
How long will it take?
How are we going to organize our society?

These questions provided a framework for daily group work. Each group made their own decisions regarding how they would address each question. For example, some groups chose to divvy up the work while some chose to address each question as a group.

These beginning questions led to other questions that emerged as groups worked in developing their communities. For example, one group, which had chosen to establish their community under the ocean, determined that they needed to know about the topography and geologic features of the ocean floor (e.g., underwater mountains, geothermal vents, fault lines). As a result of these naturally emerging questions, each group determined their own research agenda.

In addition to the beginning questions, the team decided that each group would address the following: shelter, educational system, energy sources, governmental and economic systems, community residents, the creation of a constitution and a flag.

The following are work samples from a group of four girls who chose to locate their community of the future in an underwater bubble (Aquadome). Examples include responses to beginning questions, sample journal entries, a Daily Group Plan sheet (see Figures 10.1a and 10.1b), and a Group Evaluation sheet (see Figure 10.2).

## GROUP PLANNING GUIDE
### A McHome Team Creation

GROUP # 12                                          Date: 5-4-93

NAMES: Sue, Collie, Sharon, Trish

| Goal(s) for Today: | How we're going to get there, what to take. What form of gov't. and how it is organized. |

| Done? | WHAT IS TO BE DONE? | HOW? | BY WHOM? |
|---|---|---|---|
| (Check off as you complete each task.) | (Make a list of all tasks to be done today in order to reach your above goal(s).) | (What do you need to get the job done, for example, materials, resources, etc. to meet your above goal(s)?) | (Who will be completing this task?) |
| ☐ | How to get there? more elaborate on other paper ✓ | Paper, pencil | Sue writes all contribute |
| ☐ | What to take? more elaborate on other paper | Paper, pencil | Collie writes all contribute |
| ☑ | Gov't? more elaborate on other paper | | Sharon writes all contribute |
| ☐ | Answer following?'s in essay form: 1) How are we going to get there? 2) What are we going to take? 3) What form of gov't? 4) How is it organized? | paper, pen info | each person writes 1) on question |

EVALUATION: (How did your group work today? What did you do right? What did you do wrong?)
We worked alot on the gov't plan. We couldn't do the first 2 until Sharon got back from the library and 1, 2, & 3 go with the 4th one.

REVISIONS: (If you did not reach your goal(s) today, how will you change your plan?)
Space out work. Do one thing at a time.

a

**Figure 10.1a, b.** Aquadome plan sheet.

## How to get there?

- ☑ Brainstorm types of transportation
- ☑ List types of transportation possible and how much they can carry.
- ☐ Write time it would take to get to destination in type of transportation + how much fuel needed how fast
- ☐ Once decided transportation; how many are needed, how fast, cheapest, energy saving, best for environment
- ☐ Write and draw description of the vehicle(s)
- ☐ Label the drawing and color
- ☐ Explain why the vehicle was chosen

## What to take

- ☑ Brainstorm what (sources are already there)
- ☑ Brainstorm + list things we feel necessary for survival.
- ☑ Revise the list
- ☑ Match supplies w/ jobs that we need to be filled
- ☐ Brainstorm on how many and how big and how much the vehicles can hold (for supplies taking)

## Gov't?

- ☑ Research + brainstorm the different types of possible Gov't to fit our society
- ☑ Tist the possibilities + describe
- ☑ Why it suits society
- ☐ Make an organization chart w/gov't adv. and disadv.
- ☐ Chose a form of gov't and decide how many people to take
- ☐ Decide how much power the leadership

b

## GROUP EVALUATION SHEET
### A McHome Team Creation

| | Always | 10 |
|---|---|---|
| | Mostly | 9 |
| | Sometimes | 8 |
| | Never | 0 |

Group # 1 2

| Name | TOTAL | I contributed my ideas and information | I asked others for their ideas and information | I summarized all our ideas and information | I shared my materials with teammates | I asked for help when I needed it | I helped the other members of my group learn | I made sure everyone in my group understood how to do the task | I included everyone in our work | I helped keep the group on task | I worked with my group until all came to concensus |
|---|---|---|---|---|---|---|---|---|---|---|---|
| **DATE: 5-10-93** | | | | | | | | | | | |
| Trish | 90 | 10 | 9 | 9 | 10 | 8 | 9 | 8 | 9 | 10 | 8 |
| Collie | 87 | 10 | 9 | 8 | 10 | 8 | 8 | 8 | 9 | 8 | 9 |
| Sue | 88 | 9 | 9 | 9 | 9 | 10 | 8 | 8 | 9 | 9 | 8 |
| Sharon | 85 | 9 | 8 | 8 | 10 | 8 | 8 | 8 | 10 | 8 | 8 |
| **DATE: 5-11-93** | | | | | | | | | | | |
| Trish | 92 | 10 | 9 | 8 | 10 | 9 | 9 | 9 | 9 | 9 | 10 |
| Collie | 90 | 10 | 8 | 9 | 10 | 9 | 8 | 9 | 9 | 8 | 10 |
| Sue | 92 | 9 | 10 | 9 | 9 | 10 | 10 | 8 | 8 | 10 | 9 |
| Sharon | 92 | 10 | 10 | 9 | 10 | 8 | 8 | 9 | 9 | 9 | 10 |
| **DATE: 5-12-93** | | | | | | | | | | | |
| Trish | 93 | 10 | 9 | 9 | 10 | 9 | 9 | 9 | 9 | 10 | 9 |
| Collie | 93 | 10 | 9 | 10 | 10 | 9 | 9 | 9 | 9 | 9 | 9 |
| Sue | PROBE | | | | | | | | | | |
| Sharon | 88 | 10 | 10 | 8 | 9 | 8 | 10 | 8 | 8 | 8 | 9 |
| **DATE: 5-13-93** Wk average some | | | | | | | | | | | |
| Trish | 94 / 100 | 10 | 10 | 10 | 10 | 10 | 10 | 10 | 10 | 10 | 10 |
| Collie | 92 / 97 | 10 | 10 | 10 | 10 | 9 | 9 | 9 | 10 | 10 | 10 |
| Sue | 93 / 99 | 10 | 10 | 10 | 10 | 10 | 10 | 9 | 10 | 10 | 10 |
| Sharon | 91 / 100 | 10 | 10 | 10 | 10 | 10 | 10 | 10 | 10 | 10 | 10 |
| **DATE: 5-14-93** | | | | | | | | | | | |

NADA

**Figure 10.2.** Aquadome group evaluation sheet.

Each Communities of the Future group worked to answer the beginning questions and other questions that emerged as they worked on their project. The Aquadome group's responses are as follows:

*Why are we going?* We want to start the new world, Aquadome, because we want to have a scientific study to see how real life reacts to an unreal world. We want to find out through scientific study how a steady living environment can be established in a plexiglass bubble under water.

*Who will we take and why?* The way we are presenting our "new world" to [the] public is by going around to about two hundred people and survey them. We plan to ask questions such as, if they would be willing to live under the water, reason why, and their phone number. Then we will pick one hundred people who would want to go. We would call them and go to their house with brochures about the bubble. The survey wouldn't reveil [sic] anything about the bubble. We would also give the interested and qualified people of families applications and give them an interview. Then out of the one hundred people we will pick seventy-five definate [sic] people to go. See Figure 10.3 for the Aquadome group's application form.

*What form of government will we have?* The form of government that we chose was oligarchy. We chose this form of government because we have four main people to oversee the four levels of our Aquadome. We feel that the people should be able to voice their opinions concerning their environment. We also feel that having an oligarchy will bring everyone together in a person to person relationship.

This suits our society because we have so few people. We think four people to run our society will be the best choice because not everyone is qualified to be leaders of a society.

*What economic system will we have?* Our econmy [sic] is going to be socialism. We chose socialism because we want everyone to [be] equal. We do not want there to be a middle class, an upper class, or a lower class. We also think that everyone should have equal pay. The pay will be an average middle class salary. Our resources and goods will be placed in stores for the consumers to buy.

*What will be in our constitution?* We the people of our new land, in order to form a perfect civilization, live by the following rules:

1. To be honest
2. To be trustworthy
3. To be kind to the fellow people
4. To be reliable
5. Not to have hate towards others
6. To share with others
8. Not to damage others' property

# Application

Name_____
Address_____
City_____ State_____Zip_____
DOB_____ Height_____Weight_____
Religion_____
Occupation_____
Home Phone___(____)_____
Business Phone___(____)_____
Medical Problems?_____

Reasons Why You Want To Go_____
_____
_____

Spouse"s Name_____
DOB_____ Height_____Weight_____
Religion_____
Occupation_____
Business Phone___(____)_____
Medical Problems?_____

Reasons Why You Want To Go_____
_____
_____

Number of Children_____
DOB_____ Height_____Weight_____
Religion_____
Medical Problems?_____

Reasons Why You Want To Go_____
_____

(separate sheet of paper for other children)
Number of Pets_____
Type(s)_____
Weight_____

### Family Status

How much weight does each individual plan to take:
_____
_____

How much total money do you have in your savings
account(s)?_____

How much is the yearly income within the family?_____
_____

**Figure 10.3.** Aquadome application form.

9. To be polite
10. Don't be cold-hearted and absent-minded
11. To have freedom of expression
12. At the end of every year, turn in clothes to be fixed and put back in stores to be sold
13. At the end of every year, turn in all of the money you've made to be recycled and start the process of being paid and buying things over again

*How are we going to get there?* We are leaving off the coast of Savannah, Georgia, in a hydrofoil to go to Antarctica. We are taking a hydrofoil because it is pollutant free, it runs on solar power, and it glides over the water at approximately forty miles per hour (thirty six knots). It will take us approximately four days to get to Antarctica on our hydrofoil.

When we reach Antarctica we will take our futuristic submarine down to our bubble. It runs on stored-up solar power and goes forty-six miles per hour (forty knots). It will take us twenty-two hours (approximately one day) to get to our bubble from Antarctica. To see how we mapped out our route see our map [Figure 10.4]. See Figure 10.5 for the hydrofoil and Figure 10.6 for the submarine.

**Figure 10.4.** Aquadome map.

**Figure 10.5.** Aquadome hydrofoil.

**Figure 10.6.** Aquadome submarine.

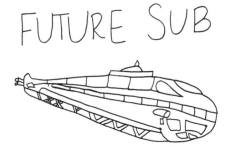

*What will we take?* Resources that are already present are water and things in the water. The resources in the water are fish, crabs, lobsters, mussels, oysters, mollusks, octopi, and shrimp. There may be some that we are not aware of.

The resources that we need to take with us are meat, vegetables, fruit, clothing, shelter, and clean air. We also need soil, dirt, seeds, honeybees, worms, etc., for the Agriculture Room.

When we go on our trip, there will be certain things we will be allowed to take. We will be allowed to take the basic necessities such as beds, couches, tables, tv's [sic], vcr's [sic], dressers, plants, rugs, and any other lightweight items that would not exceed the weight limit.

There will be a six-hundred pound limit for each individual person. Each individual will be allowed to bring pets as desired.

We will also be bringing the necessary supplies needed for our stores, hospitols [sic], churches, schools, town hall, restaurants, and any other activities we hold.

We also need to bring 500 honeybees to pollinate our plants on the agriculture level. We need to bring 500 earthworms to help break up the soil. We will also bring irridation [sic] machine to remove bacteria from our food and other goods.

Reflecting daily in their journals helped students to practice Skills Group 3. Students were to individually evaluate their work in light of group goals. They had to think about what kind of work had been done, how these tasks had helped accomplish group goals, and what could have been done better. The following are sample entries from the Aquadome group.

### [5/3/93] GROUP MEMBER RESPONSE

Today, we got a lot more done than was planned. We made a top view of our bubble and started coloring it. We finished early. I feel we finished early because we rushed through it. [We should] not [be] rushing, making it bad work, just not include every single detail. We wrote sloppy since we're gonna type it anyways [sic]. I need to pay attention more to the whole group. Trish left at some point in time. While Sue, Sharon, and myself we [sic] discussed names for our places in our bubble. We didn't know where she was. We figured she just got up and left w/o saying anything, when actually, she wrote a note that we later found.

### [5/3/93] GROUP MEMBER RESPONSE

Today we made top view pictures of every part of the bubble. We made applications for going, and determined who was going and decided exactly [sic] what you could take. We also added some necessary things to the plan for the bubble.

We competed [sic] all of our things to do. We got alot [sic] more than we thought done. I left the room to go help the new girl on the computer. I left a note but nobody saw it.

I could have took [sic] my time and done a neater job on my tasks instead of rushing through it and not going over it or revising it as much as needed.

### [5/4/93] GROUP MEMBER RESPONSE

1. Make a list of what I did yesterday (5-3-93).
2. Tell how each of these things helped my group reach its goal(s).
3. Write how much time it took for each task and total it.

| Task | How it helped accomplish the group's goals | Time it took (min) |
|------|---------------------------------------------|--------------------|
| Determined who we will take | It helped so we could get exactly how many people to take to finish their projects | 20 min |
| Why we are taking them | This helped us to determine how to make an application | 15 min |
| Made application | Helped to narrow down who could go | 10–15 min |
| Wrote what we were taking | Helped us to answer the weight limit people could bring | 15 min |
| Writing what's there and naming | Determined how many floors to have, what floors, what kind of people we needed for jobs | 20 min |
| | | Total: 80–85 min |

{WHAT I COULD HAVE DONE (BE SPECIFIC) TO USE MY TIME BETTER.

I could've elaborated more, and takin' [sic] more time to think through. We went so fast because everyone else goes back & puts it in final draft and we slop through it because we're going to type it.

*[5/4/93] GROUP MEMBER RESPONSE*

1. Make a list of what I did yesterday (5-3-93).
2. Tell how each of these things helped my group reach its goal(s).
3. Write how much time it took for each task and total it.

| Task | How it helped accomplish group goals | Time it took |
|------|--------------------------------------|--------------|
| Drew top-view pictures of each section of the bubble | Help's our group make the blueprints (the "rough" blueprints) | About 20 min |
| Listed what people needed to take on trip | Helped us to answer "who" we would take | About 10 min |
| Made an application | To help us decide who & how many we're taking & how much | About 15 min |
| Determined total # of people going | To help us on deciding weight | About 15 min |
| Determined & named what was going to be in the bubble | Help us to [know] how big the bubble is & what kind of people needed | 20 min |
| | | Total: 80 min |

*[5/6/93] GROUP MEMBER RESPONSE*

SKILLS THAT I HAVE THAT HELP MY GROUP

Some skills that I think I have that help my group are that I'm creative and I ponder on ideas. I can be organized at times but not often. I can also be very elaborate at times. I can solve problems, too.

SKILLS I NEED TO WORK ON TO HELP MY GROUP

Some skills that I feel I need to work on to help my group are to know when to be serious and when to goof off. We can be silly alot [sic] sometimes. We need to be quieter. We need to stay on one assignment and not switch if it gets boring. We need to stay on task and be nicer to our fellow peers.

*[5/6/93] GROUP MEMBER RESPONSE*

I have the skills to draw. This helps our group to do drawings. I can be organized and arrange materials so they're easier to find. I have good typing skills to help type our final form assignments. I'm creative and help produce new and neat ideas for our project.

I need to work on being on task more. This would help our group to finish assignments quicker and easier. I also need to work on being more serious and not goofing off when we need to get something done in a cirtain [sic] amount of time. We need to all work together. But we already do that!

*[5/11/93] GROUP MEMBER RESPONSE*

TODAY I ...

- voted for the transportation/this helped our group to decide what source of transportation is final
- helped get the longitude and latitude for locational map (looked on big map)/this helped our group to know exactally [sic] where our bubble is
- discussed and brainstormed depth of water and how far beneth [sic] the surface of the water the bubble would be and how far the sub could go/this helped our group to decide what our bubble would be made of and what sub to take
- discussed advantages and disadvantages of using plexiglass and/or steel for our bubble/this helped us to determine what to use for our bubble
- discussed and brainstormed ideas for submarine/this helped us to decide what sub would be best for situation

*[5/17/93] GROUP MEMBER RESPONSE*

TODAY ...

I helped to scale the drawings. We had to figure out how many miles across it was at each level. We measured everything including the hydroelectric power plant and air supply! We wanted to type the stuff on the computer but we couldn't because we started late. There were computer dificulties [sic].

Our group works well with each other even though we get off track alot [sic] but everything gets done.

In order to demonstrate Skills Group 4 (imagine, generate, and produce new ideas, solutions, or products), students prepared scaled drawings and three-dimensional models of their communities. We distributed an assessment list for a three-dimensional model and went over with our students each element. They elected to use this "ready-made" list rather than creating a rubric specifically for Skills Group 4. This list was used by the students as a guide to help them create their models as well as their final assessment tool. Students also helped assign weights for each element of the list.

The following is the Aquadome group's descriptions of the interior of their "bubble."

### Environment of Bubble

Our bubble has a nice fall-like climate all year 'round. We believe that the bubble has a very nice and comfortable temperture [sic], we will have a slight breeze. We will have a night and day like on land. We slowly dim the main lights, starting around 8 o'clock. We will not dim residental [sic] or commercial lights. With the lights dimmed it is like a night in a community.

### What to Look For

In our bubble we have four different levels. We will split things up between the levels.

On the first floor we have a hospital, two churches, two schools, a daycare, a town hall, and a park. On the second floor we have the living area. On the third floor we have the stores. We have a clothing store, a shoe store, a grocery store, and the restaraunts [sic]. On the fourth floor we have the fishing and agricultural areas, the hydroelectric power plant entrance and the air machine. We also have an irridation [sic] to remove bacteria from food, water, and clothing. On all floors we have the elevator and emergency stairs entrance and exits.

*Dimension Specifications*
Level 1: 900 feet around
Level 2: 1350 feet around
Level 3: 1125 feet around
Level 4: 562.5 feet around

*Hydroelectric Power Plant:*
- 675 feet across; 337.5 feet wide
- Pool of excess water (canals) 150–100 feet
- Control deck 20 x 20 feet
- Power box 12 x 12 feet
- Spinning wheel 75 x 20 feet
- Tunnel to let the water in & go to bubble 4 x 6 feet
- Slope 50 feet, sloping down to 15 feet

*Air Supply:*
- 562.5 x 225 feet
- Air tube 10 feet around
- Pressure meter 6 x 3 feet
- Air filter 225 x 75 feet
- Air fan 112.5 feet around
- Air tube to bubble, 10 feet around

This group also made detailed drawings of each of the four levels of their bubble as well as drawings of the laundry, air supply, and hydroelectric power plant. Each level was scaled according to its position in the bubble (see Figures 10.7, 10.8a, 10.8b, 10.9, 10.10, 10.11, and 10.12).

The actual three-dimensional model for the Aquadome group consisted of four circular figures representing the four levels. They made houses, trees, gardens, paths, and food-supply areas.

Groups presented for approximately 15 minutes and then answered questions. We graded each presentation using the Assessment List. See Figure 10.13 for the completed Assessment List for the Aquadome group.

During final presentations, groups shared details of where their communities were located, why they were located there, how they got there, their government and economic system, their constitution, and details of their three-dimensional model. For example, the Aquadome group wanted to conduct research to see how "real life reacts to an unreal world." This group chose an oligarchy form of government because "not everyone is qualified to be leaders of a society." The application form for the Aquadome group further revealed their thought processes. For example, they knew that the Aquadome could only hold so much weight, so they asked prospective applicants for the weight of family members, pets, and personal baggage. They

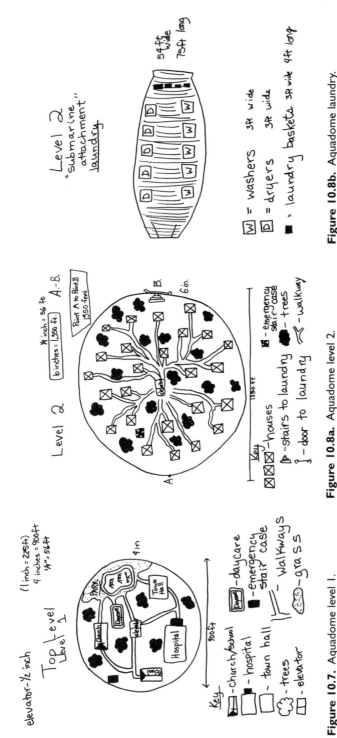

elevator-½ inch

(1 inch = 225ft)
4 inches = 900ft
¼" = 56ft

Top Level
Level 1

4 in

900ft

Key
▯ -church/school
▯ -hospital
▢ - town hall
🌳 - trees
▭ - elevator

▭ -daycare
■ -emergency
stair case
⌐ - walkways
🌿 -grass

**Figure 10.7.** Aquadome level 1.

Level 2

¼ inch = 56 ft    A - B.

6 inches = 1,550 ft

Point A to Point B
1,550 feet

B.

6 in.

1550 ft

A.

Key
⊠⊠⊠ -houses
🏠 -stairs to laundry
🚪 -door to laundry

☒ - emergency
stair case
🌳 - trees
⤳ - walkway

**Figure 10.8a.** Aquadome level 2.

Level 2
"submarine"
attachment
laundry

54 ft
wide
75ft long

W = washers    3ft wide
D = dryers     3ft wide
■ = laundry baskets 3ft wide 4ft long

**Figure 10.8b.** Aquadome laundry.

130

Level 3
5 inches = 1,125 ft
1/4 inch = 56 ft
5 in
Shoes
Clothing Store
Grocery
elevator
Sports Bar
Cafe
Kids Restaurant
1,125 ft
Key
trees
Sports bar
clothing store
shoe store
grocery store
restaurant
kids restaurant


Figure 10.9. Aquadome level 3.

Level 4
3.5 inches = 787.5 ft
every 1 inch = 225 feet
Canal
elevator
3 1/2 in
787.5 ft
– fishing area
– farming area
– special lights for growing
– elevator


Figure 10.10. Aquadome level 4.

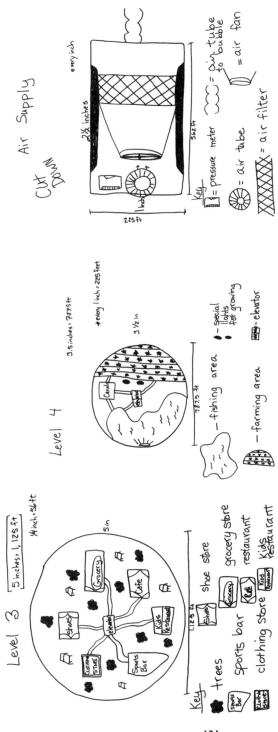

Air Supply
Cut Down
every inch
2 1/2 inches
225 ft
1 inch
562 ft
Key
= pressure meter
= air tube to bubble
= air tube
= air fan
= air filter


Figure 10.11. Aquadome air supply.

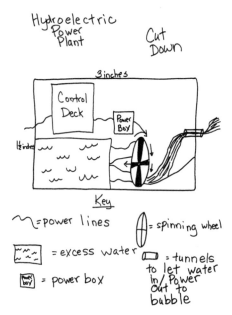

Hydroelectric
    Power
    Plant

Cut
Down

3 inches

Control
Deck

Power
Box

Birds

**Figure 10.12.** Aquadome hydro-electric power plant.

Key

∿ = power lines

◐ = spinning wheel

[≈] = excess water

▭ = tunnels
to let water
in/Power
Out to
bubble

[≋] = power box

ELEMENT
ASSESSMENT   Group #12

| | Points Possible | Earned |
|---|---|---|
| 1. A clear plan for the model is drawn. The plan shows dimensions and parts. | 20 | 20 |
| 2. The plan includes an explanation of how the model simulates the real item. The explanation includes a description of how the model differs from the real item. | 25 | 25 |
| 3. The constructed model is sturdy and simulates elements of the real item that it was intended to simulate. | 25 | 25 |
| 4. Color, labels, and other such devices are used well to clarify what the model is intended to show. | 10 | 10 |
| 5. The model is neat and presentable. | 10 | 10 |
| 6. The model is safe to use. | 10 | 10 |
| Total | 100 | 100 |

extra
+5 effort

105

**Figure 10.13.** Aquadome 3-D model assessment list.

also wanted to know the mental stability and medical problems of prospective applicants. Their constitution reflected personal attitudes and values regarding the interactions of government and society. This group was strongly in favor of an egalitarian society. The girls wanted to ensure that no one was better than anyone else in the Aquadome. They decided that, at the end of each year, everyone had to return everything they owned for equal redistribution.

When thinking about how they were going to get to their underwater site, they decided they needed to know more about submarines. They went to the library and researched the kinds of submarines that would best fit their needs. After they determined what kind of submarine they needed, they determined they needed to convert knots to miles per hour in order to answer their question, "How long will it take to get to the destination?" As they discussed possible materials for their bubble, they realized they didn't have enough information to make a decision. This led them to research materials such as Plexiglas and steel.

During the final unit, the Aquadome group along with other Communities of the Future groups were involved in creating coherent curriculum. Their learning was in depth, relevant, and personally meaningful. To achieve their goals, each group developed democratic work relationships; utilized a variety of assessments; integrated content; made connections; personalized learning; communicated effectively; developed workable schedules; and reflected.

## Chapter 11

# CONTINUING THE QUEST

We began our quest because of dissatisfaction with traditional schooling. In *Making Integrated Curriculum Work: Teachers, Students, and the Quest for Coherent Curriculum* we have shared our story of how we worked toward making our year what we believed schooling should be.

We (students and teachers) continuously worked to make our curriculum personally meaningful. Our experiences incorporated student interests and concerns, was motivating, took into account varying learning styles, and was a collaborative effort.

Our curriculum was challenging for all of us. It emphasized process and product, provided opportunities for students to take risks and learn from mistakes, promoted problem posing and problem solving, included reflection, incorporated collaboration, and utilized authentic demonstrations of learning.

This curriculum gave our students the skills and knowledge they needed to address their current needs and concerns. It provided them with experiences in which they became responsible contributors to society. It also provided them with the skills and knowledge they could take with them into their future. The curriculum was relevant to our students.

Our curriculum was also holistic. It promoted making connections, focused on depth versus breadth, and accounted for emerging knowledge. It was appropriate for the developmental needs of our middle school students. This meant it took into account current learning theories, and students' cognitive, physical, emotional, and social needs.

Our beliefs regarding schooling were affirmed because of our experience. Yet the more we know, the more we find out what we don't know.

This realization about gaps in our own knowledge about curriculum integration led us to question, read, discuss, debate, and reflect on curriculum issues, assessment, teaming, scheduling, teaching and learning strategies, student and teacher motivation, the purpose of schooling, and ways to make teaching and learning more democratic and authentic.

We are, now more than ever, even more avid readers on these subjects as a result of our experience. The books and articles we read and discussed at the beginning of our quest focused primarily on literature current at that time. Although our quest was novel for us, we found through our current readings a long history of educators seeking better schooling for students through democracy and authentic learning. We are now exploring the historical foundations for curriculum integration as conceptualized by John Dewey, Frederick Bonser, Junius Meriam, William Kilpatrick, J. S. Tippett, Thomas Hopkins, Harold Rugg, Wilford Aikin, Roland Founce and Nelson Bossing, Rosalind Zapf, and scores of early classroom educators and their students.

Early in this century, Dewey (1916) proposed school experiences that took into account the needs and interests of students. He emphasized that these experiences should be reflective of the real world. Problem solving was central to Dewey's idea of real-world-related school experiences.

Bonser (1920) stipulated that classroom curriculum should be based on two principles:

> the aims and activities of life … [and] the nature and needs of children. …
> It is possible to organize a curriculum wholly upon the basis of *activities of life* in which children actually engage rather than in terms of *subjects* in which, as such, few are engaged. (pp. v–vi)

Meriam (1927) cautioned that the curriculum of the school should "get as close as possible to the lives of children as found in the home and in the larger community" (p. vi). He urged that the curriculum should be relevant to students now rather than later, be related to real life, and take into account the differences in students' interests and abilities. He explained the proper place for the traditional subjects: the importance lies in their ability to help students effectively solve social and practical problems. Meriam emphatically maintained that there is a difference in using a subject to illuminate/solve real-life problems and using real-life problems to learn/understand subject matter. He insisted that most educators do not know the difference.

Meriam also addressed the conflict between assessment and practice within integrated curriculum. He maintained that traditional tests are developed to discover how well students are doing in the separate subjects. This very limited view of student learning is in direct conflict with student learning that is searching for and applying knowledge and skills in the pursuit of real-world problems of personal and social concern.

Kilpatrick (1936, pp. 49–50), proposed a five-step process for curriculum development based on real-life situations:

1. Start where the child's interests now are, help him to choose the best [situation] among them, and then help these to grow into something better....
2. The second step is to analyze it [the situation], partly to set up or clarify ends, partly to get materials for the planning that comes next.
3. The third step is to make one or more plans and choose from among them, for dealing with the situation....
4. Then comes the step of putting the plan into operation ... so that if need arise revision may be made.
5. A final stage is the backward look to see what has been done and how it might be done better another time.

Kilpatrick further illuminated this process when he stated:

[What is] most to be valued is how the child, or the group, is active, dynamic, thinking, feeling, pushing ahead, moving forward physically—all these are taking place at each step and phase. And note that the process is self-directed and in general contains its own inherent testing. (p. 51)

Kilpatrick emphasized that the role of the teacher should be one of guide rather than dispenser of knowledge.

Tippett (as cited in Hopkins, 1937) maintained that evaluation methods change as a result of the relationships developed through integration. This evaluation involves "the teacher's becoming interested in the whole child, in his physical, mental, moral, and social development, and in the child's coming to look upon the teacher as a helper, a guide, a comrade" (p. 297).

Hopkins (1941) insisted that schools must foster "cooperative democratic action." Aspects of cooperative democratic action involved students and their teachers:

(1) determining the purposes to be realized; (2) formulating plans for achieving them; (3) devising methods of putting the plans effectively into operation; (4) evaluating the results in improved living; and (5) selecting new and improved purposes for continued cooperative planning and action. (pp. 7–8)

Hopkins stressed that the means by which learning occurs is of paramount importance. He insisted, "Any end which cannot be achieved by the democratic process is usually not worth achieving" (p. 6). Hopkins illustrated the consequences of failing to institute cooperative democratic action in the classroom when he stated:

The hungry rat gets his food after a short trip in the maze; the seal catches the fish tossed to him by his keeper after a five-minute performance; the child receives the approval of the teacher after a 15-minute spelling lesson or a few hours of work on some project. When the performance is over the tension is released until it is again stimulated by some outside force. There is no deep-seated internal need in the rat, the seal, or the pupil of increasingly significant quality which remains a constant propulsive force. (p. 9)

From 1933 to 1941, thirty high schools participated in a landmark research project, the Eight-Year Study. The schools redesigned their curriculums to be more responsive to the needs of students. In the most progressive schools, common problems of students became the heart of the curriculum, which was called "core." The term *core curriculum* was defined as:

A course, required by all, or nearly all students, which deals with broad problems or topics without regard to subject-matter lines. It is designed to avoid the evils of compartmentalized subject-matter by dealing with all of the aspects or implications of a problem as a unified whole. (Rugg, 1939, pp. 276–277)

In making these curricular changes, "[A]lmost all the schools were trying from the beginning of the study to find ways of breaking down the artificial barriers which unfortunately separated teacher from teacher, subject from subject" (Aikin, 1942, p. 52). The results of the study showed that students from these high schools did as well as, or better than, their counterparts in other college preparatory schools on every measure. As it turned out, "[S]tudents from the schools whose pattern of program differed most from the conventional were very distinctly superior to those from the more conventional type of school" (Aikin, 1942, p. 150).

Faunce and Bossing (1951) also proposed a core curriculum. These scholars advocated experience-learning as "consistent with the kind of behavior competencies needed in our democratic society" (p. v), which they insisted was the ability to solve problems. They recommended doing away with the separate subjects and developing the curriculum around "problems of personal and societal significance so that each pupil will develop the ability to confront every problem situation calmly and critically" (p. 72). They believed that it is in the solving of real problems that youngsters learn the vital skills of living in a democratic society.

Zapf (1959) recognized the importance of young people experiencing democracy within the classroom. She offered practical advice on how to structure a democratic classroom: determining problems for study, identifying appropriate skills and attitudes to demonstrate, and specifying techniques for learning to work together.

Relating these historical accounts to our quest for coherent curriculum has added another dimension to our understanding of curriculum integration. Taking into account our deeper understanding and McHome Team experiences, there are several things we would do differently next time.

Not all of our students and parents were convinced that curriculum integration was the best approach to schooling. Next time we would share the rich history and research that supports curriculum integration and how and why it is better for meeting the needs of students. We would provide articles to read and set up forums for discussion. We would engage in more collaboration with parents regarding what goals they have for their child's education.

Not everyone embraced the idea of a democratic classroom. Some students, especially those who had learned to do well within traditional structures of schooling, were uncomfortable with some aspects of our curriculum. These students were more comfortable with teachers directing every lesson, rather than accepting responsibility for their own learning. Some students were also unhappy with the fact that democratic education takes more time. It requires listening, debating, withholding judgment until all opinions are voiced, making decisions, accepting responsibility, and tolerating ambiguity. Because we all had varying ideas about what democracy and living democratically is or ought to be, the next time we would discuss these ideas more often. At the beginning of the school year we would make time to flesh out these ideas and concepts. We (students and teachers) might pose questions such as the following: What does democracy mean? What does living democratically at home and at school mean? What is my role as an individual or as part of a group in relationship to democratic living? What responsibilities go along with democratic living? What structures support democratic living? What are obstacles to democratic living? What are the implications for schooling and living democratically? What place does democratic living have in our team goals? What is the purpose of schooling? Answering such questions would require us to share, debate, analyze, clarify, and expand our thinking. We would then decide, democratically, how we could incorporate our shared conceptions of democracy and democratic living in our lives, in school, and outside of school. Throughout the school year we would revisit these questions and pose additional ones.

Sometimes we found ourselves talking too much and not letting our students voice their opinions enough. It was also easy to fall into our old teacher role and provide answers. We needed to listen to our students more. Sometimes we thought we understood what students wanted and we misinterpreted them. Next time, we would work on communication strategies to clarify ideas and promote understanding. These strategies would include more restatement of student ideas, asking other students for clarification, and group processing.

Time was often problematic. Although our students understood that it would take time to work collaboratively, they were impatient. It took time to come to consensus, develop action plans, codevelop units, and so on. Next time, we would discuss the tension between wanting to have democratic decision making and students' feelings of restlessness.

Some of our students and parents were concerned they might not be learning what they needed for high school. Next time, to help alleviate this concern, we would regularly have students identify the skills and knowledge they were learning. We would keep a running list under separate subject headings and keep it on display so that we would constantly be reminded of what and how much we were learning. We would also bring in members of the business community to talk about the kinds of skills and knowledge (i.e., problem identification, problem solving, teamwork) that are needed in the working world to further emphasize the relevance of what we are learning.

Because curriculum integration was new for us, we felt more comfortable having separate math classes for several reasons. Our students were on varying math levels (geometry, prealgebra, algebra, general math). Because mathematics coursework is sequential in nature, we didn't feel confident we would address each student's particular needs. In addition, parents in our community were more concerned about their child's math placement in high school than any other placement. Next time, we would consciously look for ways to use mathematics skills and knowledge in the thematic units.

Assessment sometimes was an issue on the McHome Team. Not only was curriculum integration new to us all, the use of alternative assessments was new to many of our students. Next time, we would provide more opportunities for students to reflect on and critique their work, individually and in groups. This might be done in student-led conferences. In these conferences students would share examples of what and how they were learning with us and with their parents. Our students wanted more traditional assessments. Next time, we would provide more of a balance between traditional and alternative assessments.

Sometimes our students did not have an audience beyond our classroom for their work. It was important for them to have their work recognized not only by their peers and teachers, but by others as well. Next time, we would utilize our community as an audience. We would encourage our students to engage in more community service work and have that work publicly recognized.

Although it wasn't an issue for us (teachers), some educators might find it difficult to embrace curriculum integration as their total program. That's okay. It doesn't have to be "all or nothing." Some students and teachers are ready for a whole year and some are ready for just a unit or two. It looks different in every classroom and every year.

One of our students summed up what he felt about curriculum integration: "I like integrated curriculum because it's more fun than just regular class, just like that mixed juice, Twister, with the mixed fruits." Curriculum integration *is* more fun than traditional schooling. It is also more relevant and meaningful for students and teachers and it provides the *coherence* needed for middle school curriculum.

# References

Aikin, W. M. (1942). *The story of the eight-year study*. New York: Harper & Brothers.

Alexander, W. (Spring 1995). 2-teacher teams promote integrative curriculum. *Middle Ground*, 6–7.

Armstrong, T. (1994). *Multiple intelligences in the classroom*. Alexandria, VA: Association for Supervision and Curriculum Development.

Beane, J. A. (1990). *A middle school curriculum: From rhetoric to reality*. Columbus, OH: National Middle School Association.

Beane, J. A. (1991). Middle school: The natural home of integrated curriculum. *Educational Leadership, 49*(2), 9–13.

Beane, J. A. (1992). Turning the floor over: Reflections on a middle school curriculum. *Middle School Journal, 23*(3), 34–40.

Beane, J, A. (1993). Research and evaluation for a "new" curriculum. *Research in Middle Level Education, 16*(2), 1–6.

Beane, J. A. (1995a). Curriculum integration and the disciplines of knowledge. *Phi Delta Kappan, 76*, 616–622.

Beane, J. A. (Ed.). (1995b). *Toward a coherent curriculum: 1995 ASCD Yearbook*. Alexandria, VA: Association for Supervision and Curriculum Development.

Bonser, F. G. (1920). *The elementary school curriculum*. New York: The Macmillan Company.

Brandt, R. (1991). On interdisciplinary curriculum: A conversation with Heidi Hayes Jacobs. *Educational Leadership, 49*(2), 24–26.

Brandt, R. (1992). On performance assessment: A conversation with Grant Wiggins. *Educational Leadership, 50(8)*, 35–37.

Brooks, J. G., & Brooks, M. G. (1993). *In search of understanding: The case for constructivist classrooms*. Alexandria, VA: Association for Supervision and Curriculum Development.

Capelluti, J., & Brazee, E. N. (1992). Middle level curriculum: Making sense. *Middle School Journal, 23*(3), 11–15.

Carnegie Council on Adolescent Development. (1989). *Turning points: Preparing American youth for the 21st century*. Washington, DC: Carnegie Corporation.

Clark, C., & Peterson, P. (1986). Teachers' thought processes. In M. C. Wittrock (Ed.), *Handbook of research on teaching* (3rd edition, pp. 255–296). New York: Macmillan.

Crichton, M. (1990). *Jurassic Park*. New York: Ballantine Books.

Dana, T. M., & Tippins, D. J. (1993). Considering alternative assessments for middle level learners. *Middle School Journal, 25*(2), 3–5.

Dewey, J. (1915). *The school and society* (rev. ed.). Chicago: University of Chicago Press.

Dewey, J. (1916). *Democracy and education*. New York: The Macmillan Company.

Dewey, J. (1938). *Experience and education*. Bloomington, IN: Kappa Delta Pi.

Dewey, J. (1990). *The school and society. The child and the curriculum*. (Expanded edition). Chicago: The University of Chicago Press.

Faunce, R. C., & Bossing, N. L. (1951). *Developing the core curriculum*. New York. Prentice-Hall, Inc.

Fogarty, R. (1991). Ten ways to integrate curriculum. *Educational Leadership, 49*(2), 61–65.

Gardner, H. (1993). *Multiple intelligences: The theory in practice*. New York: Basic Books.

Gehrke, N. (1991). Explorations of teachers' development of integrative curriculum. *Journal of Curriculum & Supervision, 6*(2), 107–117.

Glasser, M. (1986). *Control theory in the classroom*. New York: Harper & Row, Inc.

Hopkins, L. T., et al. (1937). *Integration-its meaning and application*. New York: D. Appleton-Century Company.

Hopkins, L. T. (1941). *Interaction: The democratic process*. Boston: D. C. Heath and Company.

Jacobs, H. H. (ed). (1989). *Interdisciplinary curriculum: Design and implementation*. Alexandria, VA: Association for Supervision and Curriculum Development.

Jacobs, H. H. (1991). Planning for curriculum integration. *Educational Leadership, 49*(2), 27–28.

Kilpatrick, W. H. (1936). *Remaking the curriculum*. New York: Newson and Company.

Lewis, B. A. (1991). *The kid's guide to social action*. Minneapolis, MN: Free Spirit Publishing.

Lounsbury, J. H. (1991). A fresh start for the middle school curriculum. *Middle School Journal, 23*(2), 3–7.

Merenbloom, E. Y. (1991). *The team process: A handbook for teachers* (3rd ed.). Columbus, OH: National Middle School Association.

Meriam, J. L. (1927). *Child life and the curriculum*. New York: World Book Company.

Middle Level Curriculum Project (1991). Middle level curriculum: The search of self and social meaning. *Middle School Journal, 23*(2), 29–35.

Pate, P. E., Homestead, E., & McGinnis, K. (1993). Designing rubrics for authentic assessment. *Middle School Journal, 25*(2), 25–27.

Pate, P. E., Mizelle, N., Hart, L. E., Jordan, J., Matthews, R., Matthews, S., Scott, V., & Brantley, V. (1993). The delta project: A three-year longitudinal study of middle school change. *The Middle School Journal, 25*(1), 24–27.

Pate, P. E., Homestead, E. R., & McGinnis, K. L. (1995). Student and teacher co-created integrated curriculum. In Y. Siu-Runyan, & C. V. Faircloth (Eds.), *Beyond separate subjects: Integrative learning at the middle level* (pp. 117–125). Norwood, MA: Christopher-Gordon Publishers, Inc.

Rugg, H. (Ed.). (1939). *Democracy and the curriculum: The life and program of the American school (Third Yearbook of the John Dewey Society)*. New York: D. Appleton-Century Company.

Schlechty, P. (1991). *Schools for the 21st century*. San Francisco: Josse-Bass.

Sebranek, P., Meyer, V., & Kemper, D. (1990). *Write Source 2000*. Burlington, WI: Write Source Educational Publishing House.

Spady, W. G., & Marshall, K. J. (1991). Beyond traditional outcome-based education. *Educational Leadership, 49*(2), 67–72.

Tanner, J. M. (1972). Sequence, tempo, and individual variation in growth and development of boys and girls aged twelve to sixteen. In J. Kagan and R. Coles (Eds.), *12 to 16: Early adolescence* (pp. 1–24). New York: W. W. Norton & Company, Inc.

Tiedt, P. L., & Tiedt, I. M. (1986). *Multicultural teaching: A handbook of activities, information and resources* (2nd ed.). Boston: Allyn & Bacon.

Toepfer, C. F., Jr. (1992a). Curriculum for identity: A middle level education obligation. *Middle School Journal, 23*(3), 11–15.

Toepfer, C. F., Jr. (1992b). Middle level school curriculum: Defining the elusive. In J. L. Irvin (Ed.), *Transforming middle level education: Perspectives and possibilities* (pp. 205–243). Needham Heights, MA: Allyn and Bacon.

Vars, G. F. (1991). Integrated curriculum in historical perspective. *Educational Leadership, 49*(2), 14–15.

Vars, G. F., & Beane, J. (1994). *Critical issues in curriculum integration.* Paper presented at the National Middle School Association Annual Convention, Cincinnati, OH.

Vygotsky, L. S. (1978). *Mind in society: The development of higher mental processes.* Cambridge, MA: Harvard University Press.

Wiggins, G. (1992). Creating tests worth taking. *Educational Leadership, 50*(8), 26–33.

Wigginton, E. (1986). *Sometimes a shining moment: The foxfire experience.* Garden City, NY: Anchor Press/Doubleday.

Yinger, R. J. (1980). A study of teacher planning. *The Elementary School Journal, 80,* 107–127.

Zapf, R. M. (1959). *Democratic Processes in the secondary classroom.* Englewood Cliffs, NJ: Prentice-Hall, Inc.

# Index

## A

Aikin, W. M., 135, 137
Alexander, W., 75
Aquadome community work sample
   application form, 122
   daily group plan sheet, 117–119
   group evaluation sheet, 120
   journal entries, 125–128
   map, 123
   models, 128–133
Armstrong, T., 32

## B

Beane, J. A., 1, 2, 7, 10, 30, 31, 47
Bonser, F. G., 135
Bossing, N. L., 135, 137
Brainstorming strategy, 60–61
Brandt, R., 1
Brazee, E. N., 2
Brooks, J. G., 7
Brooks, M. G., 7

## C

Capelluti, J., 1
Carnegie Council on Adolescent
   Development, 2, 10
Clark, C., 6
Class periods, traditional, 1
Classroom assessment, 32–33, 139
Classroom organization, 79
Class schedules, 78
Communication
   parent, 70–71
   student, 68–73
   teacher, 74
Communities of the Future unit
   Aquadome, 117–133
   community determination, 114–115
   content, 4–5, 58–59, 111–114
   development and presentation,
      115–117
   initial preparation, 109–111
Content integration
   in curriculum, 47–48

   modeling, 48–53
   in thematic units, 53–59
Crichton, M., 4, 57
Curriculum
   characteristics, 134–135
   design process, 33–37, 49–53
   integration, 3, 7–9, 46–48, 139

## D

Daily group plan sheet, Aquadome
   work sample, 117–119
Dana, T. M., 31
Data retrieval chart strategy, 64–65
Delta Team, 2
Democratic classroom
   definition, 16–17
   grading policy, 24–27
   group processing, 23–24
   group-work guidelines, 27
   management plan, 17–23
   participation in, 15
   student acceptance, 138
   and student concerns, 28
Designing down unit plan
   example, 34
   student comments, 52–53
   student preparation, 36–37
Detention form, in McHome Team
   Management Plan, 22
Dewey, J., 2, 9, 135

## E

Education
   middle school, 6–7, 10
   multicultural, 9
Eight-Year Study, 137
English as a Second Language (ESL),
   78
Essential Components of a Coherent
   Curriculum, 107

## F

Faunce, R. C., 135, 137
Fogarty, R., 2

G
Gardner, H., 32
Gehrke, N., 74
Glasser, M., 2
Good student model, 18–19
Grading policy
    and redoing assignments, 25–27
    teacher-imposed, 24–25
Group evaluation sheet, Aquadome
    work sample, 120
Group norms, 24
Group processing, 23–24
Group-work guidelines, 27

H
Homestead, E., 38
Hopkins, L. T., 135, 136
Human and Civil Rights and
        Responsibilities unit
    content, 4
    and content integration, 56–57
    development, 109
    pedagogy, 60–67
Human Interactions and the
        Environment unit
    content, 4
    and content integration, 55–56
    development, 108–109
    lesson preparation, 36–37
Human Interactions unit
    content, 4
    and content integration, 53–54
    development, 108
Human Migration unit
    content, 4
    development, 108

I
Interviews, student, 89–90

J
Jacobs, H. H., 2
Jigsaw strategy, 64
Journals
    student, 82–89, 125–128
    teacher, 81–82
*Jurassic Park* (Crichton), 4, 57, 109

Kemper, D., 80
*The Kid's Guide to Social Action*
    (Lewis), 71

Kilpatrick, W. H., 135, 136
Knowledge, acquisition skills, 49

L
Leadership unit, and content integration,
        57–58
Learning
    active, 16, 36
    activities for, 35–36
    concerns about, 139
    knowledge acquisition skills, 49
    and personal ownership, 29
    process of, 7
Lewis, B. A., 71
Life roles, preparation for, 31
Lounsbury, J. H., 2

M
Marshall, K. J., 2
McGinnis, K., 38
McGinnis-Homestead (McHome) Team
    assessment, 40, 42–43
    classroom organization, 79
    class schedules, 78
    democracy on, 17
    instructional program changes, 33
    long-term goals, 109
    parent communication, 70–71
    population, 3
    rights and responsibilities, 61–62
    size, 76
    student communication, 68–70
    team teaching, 77–78
    two-teacher team, 75–77
McHome Team Management Plan
    creation, 17
    good student model, 18–19
    improvement plan in, 20–21
    warnings in, 20–23
Merenbloom, E. Y., 2
Meriam, J. L., 135
Meyer, V., 80
Middle Level Curriculum Project, 10
Middle school
    education, 6–7, 10
    student differences, 31–32
*A Middle School Curriculum: From
        Rhetoric to Reality* (Beane), 2, 10
Models
    Aquadome community, 128–133
    content integration, 48–53

good student, 18–19
  Teachers' Thought and Action, 6
Motivation, and curriculum integration,
    8
Multicultural education, 9

**P**
Parent communication, 70–71
Pate, P. E., 38
Performance assessment
  Aquadome community work sample,
    129, 132
  in curriculum design, 35, 49–50
Personal ownership, and learning, 29
Peterson, P., 6
Problem solving
  collaborative strategy, 67
  in curriculum design, 35

**Q**
Questions
  in curriculum design, 35, 49
  for student reflection, 90–98,
    102–106

**R**
Reflection process
  in coherent curriculum, 5
  in group processing, 23–24
  individual and group interviews,
    89–90
  quiz, 93–96
  student-initiated team meeting,
    101–102
  student journals, 82–89
  student questionnaire, 90–93, 96–98,
    102–106
  student response essay, 98–101
  teacher discussion, 106–107
  teacher journal, 81–82
Resources, in curriculum design, 36,
    50–52
Response essay, student, 98–101
Rising Eighth-Grade Surveys, 49
Rubrics
  creation, 38–40
  guidelines for, 38
  student perspectives on, 45
Rugg, H., 135, 137

**S**
Schlechty, P., 2
School-day schedule, 3
Sebranek, P., 80
Simulation strategy, 66
Spady, W. G., 2
Storytelling strategy, 63
Students
  communication, 68–73
  conferences, 22–23
  interviews, 89–90
  journal entries, 82–89
  participation, 16
  questions for reflection, 90–106
  responsibilities, 25–27
Study units, content, 4–5
Survey of Rising Eighth Graders, 10–14

**T**
Tanner, J. M., 31
Teachers
  communication, 74
  reflections, 81–82, 106–107
  roles, 43–45
Team meeting, student-initiated,
    101–102
Team size, 76
Team teaching, 77–78
Themes, in curriculum design, 35, 49
Tiedt, I. M., 9
Tiedt, P. L., 9
Tippett, J. S., 135, 136
Tippins, D. J., 31
Toepfer, C. F., Jr., 2, 31
Two-teacher team, 75–77

**V**
Vars, G. F., 2, 30
Vygotsky, L. S., 7

**W**
Wiggins, G., 2
Wigginton, E., 2
*Write Source 2000* (Sebranek, Meyer,
    Kemper), 80

**Y**
Yinger, R. J., 7

**Z**
Zapf, R. M., 135, 137

# About the Authors

**P. ELIZABETH PATE** is an Associate Professor and Program Area Head in the Elementary Education Department, Middle School Program, at The University of Georgia. She completed her Ph.D. in Curriculum and Instruction at Texas A & M University in 1989. Prior to graduate school, she taught at the elementary and middle school levels. She has contributed chapters and articles to a variety of books and journals. Dr. Pate has spoken at numerous international, national, state, and local conferences, been a consultant for educational projects in the United States, and served in various capacities for several professional associations.

**ELAINE HOMESTEAD** has 17 years of teaching experience in grades five through eight in departmentalized, self-contained, interdisciplinary, and integrated settings. She has coauthored several professional publications, presented workshops and papers, and consulted on various topics relating to middle school education, such as strategy instruction, curriculum integration, authentic assessment, democratic classrooms, collaborative curriculum planning, infusion of economics into the social studies, and integration of technology into curriculum and instruction. She is currently a graduate assistant in the Middle School Program at The University of Georgia where she is working toward a Ph.D. in Middle School Education.

**KAREN MCGINNIS** is a teacher at Richard Hull Middle School in Duluth, Georgia, a suburb of Atlanta. She has 8 years of experience in middle grades education in departmentalized, exploratory, interdisciplinary, and integrated settings. She is currently working in sixth, seventh, and eighth grades to establish a coherent curriculum with the students through a literature-based program. Karen has coauthored other publications including a chapter in ASCD's 1995 Yearbook *Toward a Coherent Curriculum,* a chapter in Yvonne Siu-Runyan and C. Victoria Faircloth's 1995 book *Beyond Separate Subjects: Integrative Learning at the Middle Level,* and two articles in the *Middle School Journal.* Karen has spoken at numerous national and local conferences on curriculum integration and has worked with teachers from several schools in the middle Georgia area to learn how to effectively develop integrated curriculum components. In 1994, she was awarded a Masters in Education in Middle Grades Education from the University of Georgia.